REFRACTED REALITIES

Navigating a Multifaceted Reflection

By Michael Shafia

REFRACTED REALITIES
Navigating a Multifaceted Reflection

Edited by George Verongos

Cover by Michael Shafia

ISBN: 979-8-218-31639-6

Preface

Embarking upon this exploration into the core of our collective social realm, this volume seeks to navigate through human behavior, culture, and societal norms with a lens refined by both academic scrutiny and personal inquiry. While emerging as a crystallization of my endeavors to navigate the complexities of collective consciousness and individual psyche, it also leans into a myriad of conversational and experiential moments throughout my life. This work strives to maintain a balance, grounding assertions in academic research while acknowledging that scholarly studies can be marshaled in support of diverse viewpoints, thereby underscoring the imperative for personal investigation into any concept presented. It serves as both a guide and a provocation, exploring how we, as individuals, sculpt and are shaped by our social structures, and encourages readers to navigate their path through the intricate tapestry of sociological understanding.

In the following pages, we set forth on a journey that intertwines academic investigation with a deeply personal exploration, subtly navigating through terrains of self-discovery and introspection. The sections may seem desultorily interconnected, exploring themes from personal struggles with identity to broader societal phenomena and philosophical

interpretations of nature. However, this seemingly erratic traversal is deliberate, aiming to weave together disparate thoughts and prompt reflections on unanticipated interconnections between diverse ideas. A portion of the motivation behind this book undeniably stems from what biologists term the 'legacy drive'—a profound, inherent desire to leave an enduring imprint, solidifying fleeting thoughts into perpetual prose. Thus, this text serves as a vessel, navigating through our shared and individual journeys within the elaborate tapestry of abstract constructs.

In the end, this book aims to shed light on the nature of our existence within the sociological structures that surround us, and to provide a meaningful framework for understanding our roles within this grand macro-organism we call society. Whether you're seeking to comprehend the world around you with greater nuance or looking for a mirror to reflect on your own experiences, I hope the insights presented here will guide and inspire you, or at the very least, evoke some modicum of critical thought.

Think of this book like it's the Disney amusement park ride *Soarin' Around the World*: we're going to teleport all over the conceptual landscape, briefly bear witness to the passing sights, and hopefully not lose our shoes in the process. Though this book will likely be far less thrilling.

Within the labyrinth of our collective consciousness, the footprints of invisible architects guide our path. Whispered echoes of their ethereal presence subtly reshape our thoughts, weaving narratives anew, as humanity waltzes on the edge of

an unseen precipice, unknowingly unified with our spectral
partners.

TABLE OF CONTENTS

PART ONE

Foundations of Consciousness and Personal Development

CHAPTER ONE

Contextualizing Our Consciousness

While it's common to celebrate our species for its intelligence, this assessment warrants closer scrutiny. Our cognitive abilities, impressive as they may be, are deeply contextual, primarily evolved to navigate the specific ecosystems we inhabit. It is not so much that we are universally "smart," but rather that our brains have developed to serve very specific, circumstantially relevant functions within our own environmental frameworks, particularly society itself. Perhaps "cognitively agnostic" is a better way to describe the nature of the human brain, since the features of intelligence may not be readily known until prompted by experience. In this context, we might consider ourselves as initially born "tabula rasa"—a term originating from Latin that means "blank slate." Philosophers like John Locke proposed the tabula rasa theory, suggesting that individuals are born without any preconceived notions, ideas, or personality traits. It's only through our lived experiences and interactions with our

environment that we acquire knowledge, beliefs, behaviors, and attributes. Just as a raw block of marble can be sculpted and chiseled into an elegant, recognizable form, our initial blank slate gets molded and shaped by the diverse influences and experiences we encounter.

Drawing a parallel from the realm of quantum mechanics, our development might also resonate with the uncertainty principle, a phenomenon conceptualized by Werner Heisenberg. This principle posits that certain pairs of properties (like position and momentum) of a particle cannot both be accurately measured at the same time. Extending this to our own growth and evolution, perhaps the true nature or potential of our intelligence and capabilities remains in flux, somewhat nebulous, until they are "observed" or activated by the world around us. Just as quantum particles seem to exist in a state of probability until they're measured or observed, our latent abilities and skills might remain dormant until they're "measured" by the unique challenges and encounters of our lives. Perhaps looking through the quantum lens provides a clearer foundation for comprehending our essence. Even with its inherent uncertainties, quantum mechanics presents quantifiable properties and values, such as spin and energy level. These allow us to craft a more tangible understanding of the foundational elements leading to the more complex and less abstract processes in the natural world. Emergent properties stemming from basic energetic or mechanical functions birth intricate interconnected systems. At the quantum level, these foundational operations pave the way for escalating levels of complexity in broader structures. Building on this idea, where

smaller components amalgamate into multifaceted wholes, we find parallels in our own nature.

From this vantage point, our individual consciousness in the context of society mirrors the role of cells within an organism. Each cell, composed of organelles and driven by molecular enzyme engagement, performs its role based on foundational biological principles with remarkable efficiency, but its perceptible understanding is confined to its immediate environment. It remains largely unaware of the broader picture the brain apprehends. Yet, it's conceivable that, on some level, there may be a form of information exchange or "consciousness" that permeates the entire organism, connecting the micro to the macro in ways we have yet to fully understand. Which leads us to contemplate a further notion: could our consciousness, our perceived intelligence, be an instance of stochastic parroting? Much like a parrot replicates human speech without truly comprehending it, our brains may echo the complexities of our environment, creating a facsimile of understanding that is as impressive as it is limited. This notion doesn't detract from our intelligence, but it provides a humbling contextualization, inviting us to appreciate the vast complexities that lie beyond our immediate understanding. As we ponder the intricacies of our own consciousness and understanding, it's worth noting the tools that shape them. Language, our primary medium of thought and communication, has undergone profound shifts, especially in our modern epoch.

At its core, semantics delves into the study of meaning within language, focusing on the significance of words,

phrases, and sentences in conveying thought, emotion, and information. The potency of language lies in the depth of meaning each word encapsulates and the shared understanding of its significance among speakers. Over time, cultural, social, and political influences mold these meanings, fostering the dynamic evolution of language. However, when the fundamental principles of semantics are overlooked or intentionally distorted, the clarity and intent of language can be jeopardized. Each word and phrase carry a rich tapestry of meanings, built upon layers of historical and cultural contexts. When the semantic clarity of these elements is obfuscated, not only do individual words suffer, but the entire framework of communication risks becoming disjointed. In essence, to truly value and utilize the might of language, a profound comprehension and appreciation of its semantic roots are essential.

One possible antidote to this linguistic distortion lies in disavowing euphemisms or any form of figurative speech, a step that may guide us towards a more harmonized comprehension of semantic consensus. Renowned Irish poet Oscar Wilde's insightful declaration that "Sarcasm is the lowest form of wit, but the highest form of intelligence" has progressively begun to resonate deeply with me, both from an observational standpoint and through the lens of lived experience.

While sarcasm could be dismissed as a languid, subversive linguistic jest, it is deployed with a keen awareness of the sociocultural norms and rules that scaffold the topic under discussion. It hence remains a testament to the wielder's sharp intellect, deftly illuminating the dualistic nature of language as both a facilitator of and a barrier to understanding, serving as

a potent reminder of the ongoing struggle to shape and be shaped by the nuanced dynamics of language in a rapidly evolving world.

To help understand the scope of the subject, it might be helpful to reassess and restructure our perspective from another point of view. Ferdinand de Saussure, a Swiss linguist from the late 19th and early 20th centuries, is often heralded as the father of modern linguistics. His revolutionary ideas laid the groundwork for structuralism in linguistics and continue to influence many disciplines, from anthropology to literary theory.

Central to Saussure's theories is the concept of the linguistic sign, which he argued is made up of two inseparable components: the signifier and the signified. The signifier refers to the physical form of the sign, such as the sounds that make up a word or the marks on a page. In contrast, the signified is the concept or meaning the sign represents in our minds. For example, in the word "tree," the sequence of letters "t-r-e-e" or the sounds associated with those letters are the signifier, while the mental image or concept of a tree is the signified.

Saussure emphasized the arbitrariness of this relationship. There's no inherent reason why the specific sequence of sounds or letters "t-r-e-e" should represent the concept of a tree, except for the fact that speakers of English have collectively agreed upon this association. Even from an etymological perspective, this arbitrary nature of linguistic signs underscores the importance of social conventions in language.

Furthermore, Saussure posited that the meaning of a sign doesn't arise from the connection between the signifier and

the signified alone. Instead, signs derive their meanings in relation to other signs within the language system. This relational characteristic suggests that no sign has an absolute meaning in isolation; it's always defined in relation to other signs.

Consider the interrelationship between the terms "hot" and "cold." At face value, "hot" might be understood as a descriptor for a high temperature. Yet, its full significance isn't merely about warmth or heat in isolation. Rather, it is intricately tied to its antonym, "cold." The very comprehension of what "hot" denotes is shaped, in part, by our understanding of what it means for something to be "cold" and vice versa. Case in point, friends of mine who grew up in Las Vegas tend to not think anything unusual of the intense heat associated with the summer season, yet when they move to California and acclimate to the more temperate climate, they tend to experience a more alarming sense of contrast once they revisit their home state. Were we to imagine a linguistic system that lacks a term for "cold," the concept of "hot" would likely shift, as its contrastive reference point would be missing. It's this relational dynamic in language—the way terms define and are defined by their counterparts—that enriches and nuances the meanings we attach to individual words. This exemplifies Saussure's notion that words, or signs, gain their significance not just from individual definitions, but from their positions and relationships within the broader linguistic structure.

Saussure's ideas fundamentally shifted the focus in linguistics from the study of historical and etymological developments to the study of language as a structured system of signs.

His notion of the signifier and signified remains a foundational concept in semiotics, the study of signs and symbols, underscoring the intricate relationship between form and meaning in language.

The dynamics of language and our relationship with it lead us to the intriguing premises of the Sapir-Whorf hypothesis. This concept, developed by American linguists Edward Sapir and Benjamin Lee Whorf, posits a reciprocal relationship between language and thought (Whorf, 1956). It is divided into two related ideas: linguistic determinism, which suggests that language shapes thought, and linguistic relativity, the notion that variations in language reflect differences in thinking.

The stronger form of the hypothesis, linguistic determinism, argues that language isn't merely a tool for expressing thought, but actually shapes and restricts the way we think. This controversial view implies that our worldview is constrained by the limitations and possibilities of our native language. Research into color perception across different cultures, for example, has shown that language may indeed influence the way we categorize and recognize colors (Kay and Kempton, 1984). Cognitive scientist Lera Boroditsky's work has further illuminated this concept, demonstrating how different languages influence thinking and perception, such as her studies on how languages structure time (Boroditsky, 2001). One could criticize the deterministic view and argue that it oversimplifies the relationship between language and cognition, ignoring non-linguistic influences on thought. However, while other factors do influence cognition, the power of language as a primary driver of thought and

perception cannot be understated, as it acts as the very framework through which we interpret the world around us.

Linguistic relativity, the milder form of the hypothesis, emphasizes the link between language and culture. It posits that language is a reflection of the unique worldview and cognitive patterns of a particular culture, thereby influencing, but not determining, thought. Evidence supporting linguistic relativity can be found in the rich variations of language structures across cultures. Inuit languages, for instance, have a multitude of words for snow and ice, reflecting the significance and nuances of frozen water in their daily life (Igor Krupnik, 2011).

The Sapir-Whorf hypothesis highlights the intricate ways in which language shapes and is shaped by our experiences, culture, and thinking. It underlines the importance of recognizing language not only as a means of communication but also as a mediator of our perception and understanding of the world. In an age where language is often weaponized and manipulated, understanding these nuanced connections may provide insights into fostering empathy, cross-cultural communication, and genuine understanding. It could even act as a path towards unmasking the distortions in our language, aligning more closely with a shared comprehension of reality.

Language, as this exploration underscores, is a living, evolving entity. It's not merely a static tool but a dynamic interplay of culture, thought, and individual expression. From Wilde's insight into the subversive power of sarcasm to the multifaceted theories of Sapir and Whorf, our exploration of

language opens a window into the human soul and the diverse landscapes of our collective existence.

The Interplay of Emotion and Cognition in Consciousness: A Neuroscience Perspective

Human thought emerges from the intricate synaptic activities within our brain. Synapses, the brain's functional units, are diverse in structure and function. Their response can change based on past usage patterns and the presence of particular biochemicals. This adaptability, known as synaptic plasticity, is essential for producing complex behaviors and forming memories. Neurotransmitters, the molecular messengers of the nervous system, bridge these synapses and enable communication between neurons, especially in areas like the emotion-linked limbic system and the language-processing cortical regions. Modern research is increasingly focused on how this synaptic adaptability shapes behaviors, especially in learning and memory. (Kandel et al., 2012).

In a related vein, the effects of hallucinogenic substances on brain activity provide another perspective through which we can explore the complex dynamics of cognition and consciousness. Hallucinogens, such as psilocybin found in psychedelic mushrooms, LSD, and DMT, often lead to deep experiences perceived as explorations of consciousness. Yet, when individuals attempt to articulate their insights afterward, they often produce vague stories instead of clear reflections. Recent brain imaging studies show that substances like psilocybin reduce activity in central brain areas, often considered hubs for information processing. The intensity of the psychedelic experience was directly linked to this decrease in activity. Moreover, psilocybin affected how key brain areas communicated with each other, suggesting that hallucinogens might alter usual brain communication patterns, leading to a more unrestricted state of thought or imagination and interference with short-term memory. (Carhart-Harris et al., 2012).

A few years ago, at an ayahuasca ceremony in the middle of the Mojave Desert, I met a diverse group of individuals from various geographical and socioeconomic backgrounds. One attendee in particular, a software engineer from San Francisco, stands out in my memory, perhaps because of the cognitive dissonance I perceived in her presence out there in the middle of nowhere. She arrived in a Maserati and possessed a "tech bohemian" type of vibe. She then proceeded to share a tale from a prior ceremony, asserting, among other things, that she managed to intuitively derive the mathematical blueprints behind the Great Pyramid of Giza and spoke of it with flowery descriptors. Though when pressed for concrete details, her explanation veered into abstraction, being unable

to describe anything of substance. Nonetheless, she held steadfast to the idea that she had tapped into some elusive wisdom.

This difficulty in articulating profound insights induced by hallucinogens could hint at the crucial role of the limbic system, our brain's emotional epicenter, in generating these feelings of understanding. Rather than stemming from our cortex's rational, cognitive processes, the sensation of "wisdom" might emerge from our more primal brain regions. This interpretation aligns with theories suggesting that our emotions, governed by limbic structures, can influence our cognition, with the cortex providing rational support for these emotions retrospectively (Damasio, 1994).

In stark contrast to the tech bohemian traveler from San Francisco, a few attendees had vastly different backgrounds and reactions to the DMT compound. One man, a lifelong resident of California's high desert, and evidently from a less privileged socioeconomic background, underwent a deeply harrowing experience. He was visibly distressed—crying, clearly in great physical discomfort, almost cataleptic at times. Unlike others, he offered no grand interpretations of his experience with ayahuasca. It appeared to be either an act of seeking penance or a desperate attempt to momentarily flee from the bleakness of his everyday existence. Many in the group shared this viewpoint, with several noting they had participated in the ceremony multiple times, sometimes as many as 10 or 12 times. This frequent participation suggested that, for some, the ceremony might serve more as a coping or understanding mechanism rather than offering long-term

solutions. Additionally, the inclination of some participants towards fringe conspiracy theories further indicated this pattern. Without sounding too judgmental, it was evident that some individuals in the group grappled with challenges in their perceptions.

Our reactions to profound experiences—such as mind-altering substance rituals—are molded by a combination of our genetic makeup that establishes our neural foundation and our environmental encounters that shape our emotions. Hallucinogenic experiences provide a unique window into this intricate interplay between emotion and cognition, revealing the profound depths and intricacies of human consciousness.

The Authentic Path to Mastery

The aphorism "fake it until you make it" permeates not only the realms of arts and entertainment but also extends its reach to virtually any field where a defined path of progression lies. The philosophy at its core espouses the idea of accelerating the transformation from novice to expert, essentially by erecting a veneer of lies or a façade to streamline this journey. The objective is to craft an illusion of success or proficiency while concurrently, albeit discreetly, cultivating the underpinning infrastructure of skill, status, or competence that lends substance to the outward persona.

Picture a fledgling producer eager to carve out a niche in the competitive world of filmmaking. The role of a producer hinges largely on relationship-building skills and the knack for orchestrating deals, in order to shepherd an idea from the scripting phase and pre-production, all the way through to post-production and distribution. Hypothetically, one could bluff their way through this complex process, maintaining an air of confidence that convinces everyone involved that they've got things under control. And sometimes, that

semblance of mastery can be just as effective as the real thing, particularly if luck is on your side. As an "Academy Award-winning" producer myself, I can vouch for the fact that even with a wealth of experience, production is often subject to unpredictable variables beyond one's control or comprehension. I could certainly use that accolade to boost my reputation, and others might regard my opinion with a certain amount of social validation, but it doesn't necessarily indicate genuine expertise on the matter of filmmaking. Sometimes the forces that surround us just happen to align with our personal intentions or goals for success, like predicting that the sun will rise, and then taking pride in the fact that Earth completed another rotation. Sure, we're all happy that the prediction was correct, but it was likely going to happen, regardless. Anyway, I digress. The point is that a dash of innate sensibility paired with a convincing show of assurance, whether it be through tokens or demeanor, can serve as a credible disguise until genuine expertise is acquired. In domains such as this, it's not so much about what you know, but what you can convince others to believe about you.

If this persona is deemed valuable by the surrounding environment, then the goal is duly achieved for practical consideration. However, if the foundational truth fails to keep pace with the lie, even the slightest stress can fracture this veneer, laying bare the impostor beneath and potentially inflicting irreversible damage to relations with peers or clients. Such duplicity is challenging to absolve and remains etched in memory. A proficient and skilled individual may harbor a persistent fear of being unmasked as an imposter, serving as a defense mechanism. Yet, the demarcation is unambiguous.

External showmanship, driven purely by self-centered motives and devoid of a sense of purpose or direction, invariably culminates in distress. It is unsustainable to feign an affinity for that which is fundamentally at odds with one's inherent sensibilities or emotional impulses, unless external rewards such as monetary gain or authority provide ample motivation. Nevertheless, even upon attaining these rewards, introspection would illuminate the troubling cognitive dissonance borne of investing considerable time and energy in maintaining a façade.

One could indeed go through the motions of a process for an extended period without truly learning from it. The value of practice, then, is void unless it's driven by a genuine fascination for the task at hand or a hitherto undiscovered natural talent. Within the grand cosmic waltz that is life, authenticity appears to have an irreplaceable role in the pursuit of true mastery and triumph. If we mechanically follow a path without passion or interest, we are unlikely to extract wisdom or improve our abilities. This is because the absence of an emotional or intellectual engagement hampers the depth of understanding and the creativity necessary for personal growth and innovation. Consequently, the act of practicing becomes a hollow routine, devoid of learning and development. Mastering a singular motion through rote muscle memory can certainly enhance dexterity specific to a particular skill. However, it's akin to having all the essential building blocks for construction but lacking the architectural vision to assemble them into something meaningful.

To relate a bit more of personal experience here, I began learning to play the bass guitar at age 14, influenced by iconic bassists like Flea and Les Claypool, among others in the funk, rock, and metal genres. Tackling the Red Hot Chili Peppers' cover of "Higher Ground" demanded countless hours and felt like a pivotal achievement at the time. When you're at that age, you don't necessarily think about the musicality of a song, just that it sounds cool, and Flea's energy while performing the song certainly added to its appeal, so these factors can have quite the influence over a child's motivation to adopt characteristics into his own sense of self. However, my enthusiasm waned sharply after gaining this minimum level of proficiency with the slap bass technique. In hindsight, I realize my efforts were fueled by an unspoken belief that greater rewards lay ahead. But when the journey started to feel more like a series of burdensome tasks with no immediate sense of satisfaction for the process, it became clear this wasn't the right path for me.

From my perspective, true proficiency and success are not the products of monotonous practice but stem from an authentic engagement with the task. When we approach something with genuine interest or natural aptitude, we are more likely to engage deeply, challenge ourselves, learn from our mistakes, and persist in the face of obstacles. As George Clinton says, "You can't fake the funk," which alludes to the idea that genuine feeling, authenticity, and soul—especially in music and performance—can't be imitated or replicated without the genuine emotion or spirit behind it. In the context of funk music, which Clinton is famously associated with, the "funk" embodies a deep, raw, soulful feeling that emanates from

genuine emotion and passion. If someone tries to replicate this without truly feeling it, the result will come across as insincere or hollow. In a broader sense, this phrase has been used to emphasize the importance of authenticity in various aspects of life. If you're not genuine in your endeavors, people can often sense it. This authenticity propels us beyond mere repetition, encouraging us to explore, experiment, and eventually excel. Within the larger cosmic confluence, authenticity acts as the pivotal force in our quest for mastery and success. By being true to ourselves and following our interests and strengths, we unlock the true potential of practice, enabling us to grow, learn, and achieve our goals.

That being said, it could be worthwhile to consider the world through a solipsistic lens, in order to help empower us to manifest more authentically, as everything would be understood solely from this singular viewpoint. If your experiential reality is all that exists, then there's no external judgment, granting you the freedom to explore and make mistakes without fearing repercussions. Within the confines of your solipsistic shell—the solipsism chrysalis phase—you have the space to grow and evolve. Once you've cultivated enough confidence in your abilities, you can then step out and showcase your skills or knowledge to the world. While remaining in this phase perpetually might not promote long-term societal equilibrium, it could serve as a therapeutic antidote to the overwhelming weight of external reality, when applied in limited intervals. The versatility of the solipsism chrysalis approach is its applicability regardless of one's stage in life.

While our bodies inevitably progress through the natural stages of aging, our consciousness doesn't always evolve at the same pace. Sometimes, it remains stunted or delayed, held back by past traumas, fears, or unprocessed experiences. But with the chrysalis methodology, one can initiate a transformative journey of the mind at any age, allowing for the maturation and development of consciousness even if the physical self has long since matured. This offers a beacon of hope and a tool for growth for anyone feeling out of sync with their inner self, irrespective of their age. It's essential to give our inner selves the necessary time to metamorphose, ensuring we don't prematurely disturb the cocoon before the transformation is fully realized, at which point we can rejoin the broader shared reality and engage the other members of society in a productive manner.

For countless individuals, childhood and adolescence weren't the nurturing crucibles of growth they should have been. External factors, family dynamics, or societal pressures may have inhibited the natural evolution of our consciousness. The solipsism chrysalis framework isn't just a tool; it's a second chance. It gifts individuals the agency to step back into the transformative journey, irrespective of their past or present circumstances, ensuring that the path to personal evolution and self-actualization remains accessible and achievable for all. This approach is a testament to the human spirit's resilience and the belief that it's never too late to become the best version of oneself.

Throughout this discussion, I've frequently invoked the notion of "manifestation." For clarity's sake, it's important to

distinguish how I'm employing this term, especially in relation to widely recognized concepts such as the Law of Attraction. That version of manifestation, when viewed within the complex web of interdependent events and causality, raises questions about its feasibility. Can one truly shape their external reality purely with thought, especially when it might conflict with another's intent? I would say that seems like a paradoxical violation of internal logic. The solipsism chrysalis offers a solution to this conundrum by suggesting that true manifestation is an internal journey. Instead of attempting to change the outer world directly, it focuses on the metamorphosis of the self. Through the process of nurturing and refining our inner world, we naturally influence our external experiences, not through sheer will against the universe's fabric, but through genuine evolution and personal transformation. Countering the premise of *The Secret* even further, we acknowledge that the emphasis isn't on seeking external validations or rewards, but rather on embracing one's true essence and potential. One doesn't "request" or "hope" for change; they embody it. This focus on self-evolution and personal growth allows us to align with the most optimized path of cosmic causality, eliminating the distractions of ego and societal definitions of success, urging one to flourish within their own unique domain and hold themselves to their personal pinnacle of excellence. It's a journey of self-discovery and self-fulfillment, unclouded by external expectations. However, this process entails much more than just the development of skill set proficiency or confidence in oneself.

Emerging from conceptual cocoon phase brings with it the gift of heightened consciousness. Just as a caterpillar

undergoes a profound evolution, developing intricate compound eyes in its butterfly form, one transitions from limited understanding to a more expansive, enlightened viewpoint. This evolution allows one to perceive the world with new-found clarity and insight, making previously obscured truths and nuances suddenly discernible. It's not just about personal growth; it's about achieving a deeper, more profound connection to the world around you, equipped with the wisdom and perspective that the chrysalis phase nurtures.

CHAPTER FOUR

Astral and Existential Origins

Let's momentarily shift away from our narrow introspection to add further understanding of reality as a whole. At our core, we're composed of particles as ancient as the big bang. Our consciousness is perhaps woven from a tapestry of panpsychist notions and the entropy of realities, both past and present. By embracing this comprehensive view, we can profoundly transform our perception of individuality and our cosmic significance. Remember, every atom within us was once part of a star that went supernova billions of years ago, scattering the essential particles that shape our current universe. This underscores our intrinsic bond with the vast expanse of the cosmos.

In a similar vein, our present consciousness can be perceived as a mosaic of past forms of primordial sentience or awareness, as it is continually shaped and reshaped by our experiences, interactions, and the collective knowledge passed down through generations. This dynamic process of consciousness evolution is a testament to our shared humanity and interconnectedness. And while our physical selves are

composed of age-old particles and our conscious minds are influenced by past energy states, we could be more than just the sum of these parts. Even though humans may be more similar than we would like to admit, each of us brings a unique interpretation to our shared experiences, a distinctive viewpoint to our collective consciousness, creating a personal narrative that is uniquely our own (at least in any time span worth considering for the purposes of this matter.) When contemplating the true essence of individuality, the concept of the spirit often emerges, present in Abrahamic and non-Abrahamic belief systems alike. This is seen as our enduring core, transcending life and death, and acting as the foundational force guiding all our decisions. Or maybe it's just some quantum coding that leads us to believe that it's all numinous free will, while the cosmic algorithm executes as it's "programmed" to do. Who can know for sure?

But giving adequate consideration to this concept can foster a profound sense of unity and connectedness, bridging the gap between the individual and the universe, and between past, present, and future consciousness. It can inspire a sense of wonder, humility, and respect for the intricate web of existence that we are all a part of.

Much like how planets and stars evolve from the foundational accretion discs in the vast cosmos, and how consciousness springs forth from its underlying physiological constituents, our functional social interactions too stem from their inherent principles of amalgamation. Success, as commonly expressed, has a propensity to flock with its like, supported by the idea that we are the average of the five people we spend

the most time with, which is frequently mentioned in self-development literature. Therefore, if one finds his or herself ensconced within a milieu lacking the characteristics and values often associated with achievement, it could serve as a prompt for personal reassessment. Gravity serves as the foundational force behind planet creation, but once life takes root on its surface, the terrain can be reimagined by more intricate forces and higher orders of complexity. Similarly, we often find ourselves sculpting and refining our own lives built from societal gravitation fields in order to derive meaningful value from our inherent circumstances, even if we have to admit that they were embarrassing or less than ideal to begin with. This is not to categorize oneself or others as "losers"—a term laden with defeatism and negativity—but to cultivate mindfulness of one's environment and its potential influences.

A wealth of research demonstrates the profound impact our social networks can have on our behaviors, beliefs, and overall life outcomes (Fowler and Christakis, 2008). This concept applies to various aspects of life, ranging from happiness and health habits to educational achievement and economic success. If self-observation within one's environment kindles dissatisfaction or an aspiration for growth, it should be interpreted as an impetus to acquire new skills, enhance existing ones, or adapt in ways that more closely align with one's personal definition of success.

Active engagement with individuals who radiate positive attitude and potential and learning from their proactive life approach can be a potent strategy for self-improvement. Indeed, mentoring relationships and the influence of "positive

deviants" within social networks can drive personal growth and behavioral change (Singhal, 2019).

Keep in mind that we are not static entities; our capacity for learning and personal development is virtually limitless, within reason (Dweck, 2006). Therefore, embrace change, strive for continuous improvement, and remember that the company we keep often reflects our internal state. As the saying goes, "Show me your friends, and I'll show you your future." We'll revisit this subject with a more practical application in a later section.

CHAPTER FIVE

The Nature of "Why"

The quest to understand the origin of the word "why" and the history of questioning is not only a linguistic endeavor but also an exploration into the very nature of human consciousness and existential thinking.

The English word "why" is derived from the Old English word "hwī," which stems from Proto-Germanic "hwī," akin to the Latin "quī" and the Sanskrit "kis." Each of these antecedents plays a role in forming questions, delving into the reasoning or cause behind an event or situation.

While we cannot pinpoint the exact moment the first human posed a question, it is conceivable that as soon as early humans developed the cognitive capacity for symbolic thought and language, they began asking questions. These rudimentary queries likely pertained to immediate needs or observations: "What is this?" "Where is that?" Over time, as cognitive capacities expanded and cultures evolved, these questions grew more abstract and profound.

The emergence of the question "why" signifies a fundamental shift in human cognition. Instead of just reacting to the world, early humans began seeking to understand it. This questioning is the bedrock of existentialism, a philosophy concerned with human existence, freedom, and the search for meaning.

With the capability to ask "why" comes the possibility of doubt, introspection, and even existential dread. This abstract suffering, or the anguish of trying to find inherent meaning in life, is a byproduct of our ability to ponder our existence. The existentialists, from Sartre to Camus, grappled with this very idea. For them, the absence of a clear answer to "why" was both a challenge and an invitation to create one's own meaning.

In essence, the birth of the question "why" ignited the flame of abstract suffering. By asking "why," humanity both burdened itself with existential uncertainty and gifted itself the freedom to seek and create meaning in the vast tapestry of existence.

The very act of questioning, epitomized by the word "why," marks a critical juncture in the evolutionary saga of life. It signifies the dawn of a fresh ecosystem—not of tangible organisms, but of intangible thoughts. While nature thrived with plants and animals, humanity introduced a new domain of life: a realm of ideas and consciousness. Historical relics, whether they be artworks, literature, or other mediums, serve as fossils of this intellectual evolution, echoing the sentience that birthed them.

As we progress into modern times, this abstract life is taking on a form that's almost autonomous, especially as we see artificial intelligence evolve. The symbiotic relationship between humans and their ideas, which once seemed inseparable, now hints at a future divergence. Perhaps, in the not-so-distant future, we'll face the evolution of the "why" in its most raw, visceral form, transcending the abstract and allowing us a direct confrontation with the essence of our existential curiosities. This eventual convergence might offer a resolution to humanity's age-old quest for understanding, merging the tangible and intangible in a dance of cosmic comprehension.

Yet, as we anticipate revelations from our evolving technological counterparts about the essence of "why," we are drawn to face a more profound, unsettling prospect: perhaps the universe isn't bound by a grand design or purpose tailored for us. Each endeavor to fathom "why" is met by a counterbalancing "why not," suggesting the universe's potential apathy to our existential inquiries. This duality serves as a stark reminder that, in our pursuit of meaning, we may be seeking answers in a cosmos that remains indifferent to our yearnings.

Imagine a scientist meticulously dissecting the behavior of particles, asking, "Why do they behave in this manner?" The universe, in its vastness and mystery, could just as validly respond with "why not?" Similarly, a philosopher may ponder on the purpose of human existence, only to confront the counter-question: "Why not exist without a clear purpose?"

This dance between "why" and "why not" can be seen in our everyday choices and scenarios. When an artist chooses a particular hue for a painting, asking, "Why this shade of blue?"

the universe might whimsically reply, "Why not that shade?" In relationships, we often search for reasons behind our feelings—why we love, why we hurt. But the universe, in its boundless wisdom or indifference, might just as easily posit, "Why not feel this way?"

The interaction between matter and antimatter, where a slight imbalance in the early universe favored matter, parallels our human interaction with the existential concepts of "why" and "why not." Just as particles like electrons and positrons annihilate upon meeting, human experience can be viewed as a constant collision of these two existential concepts. Each life event releases a flurry of "why" and "why not" charged impulses, with our subsequent actions or inactions reflecting the prevailing existential particle. Through this lens, every individual becomes a universe in microcosm, where these collisions materialize as decisions and actions, thereby affecting the tangible reality we share.

The evolution from the formless "why not" to the structured "why" draws a parallel with our own cognitive evolution, transitioning from the primal limbic responses to the advanced reasoning of the cerebral cortex. Just as the limbic system impulsively resonates with the unrestricted essence of "why not," the cerebral cortex aims to construct and comprehend, much like the "why" seeks to define and understand. This intrinsic dualism in our cognition not only embodies the spectrum of human thought but also mirrors the universe's trajectory from nebulous chaos to defined structure. This continuous confluence, in essence, shapes the trajectory of our collective human narrative.

PART TWO

Exploring Self-Improvement and Bias

CHAPTER SIX

Interplay of Cognitive Biases in the Realm of Self-Improvement

Earlier, we delved into a more abstract interpretation of the self-help concept and discussed the importance of intrinsic empowerment. Now we will examine an approach to resolving obstacles standing in the way of interpersonal development. There's a plethora of self-help literature and advisors urging you to "just go for it" or to disregard the opinions of others when pursuing your goals, asserting that rejection or failure shouldn't be taken as a serious matter, and the likelihood that those who bear witness to said failure probably won't even recall the incident after the fact. While this might be largely accurate, they often don't provide concrete statistical evidence to back their claims, even if they do bring up personal anecdotes as illustrative examples of their theories. They might also advise you to adopt the mindset of an improv actor, assuming a character role in the situation to act in a more relaxed way, in order to mitigate the anxiety of your individual "self" experiencing rejection or

embarrassment. This particular subject comes up quite a bit in the realm of dating, as young men tend to have trouble building up the courage to talk to a prospective partner. Now ideally, one would spend as much time as necessary in the solipsist chrysalis cell, in order to build the confidence necessary to talk to anyone comfortably. But for those who might be innately incapable of arriving at that state through introspection and personal development alone, there are other solutions.

As one potential remedy to this situation, I propose combining these two ideas and taking on the role of a researcher in sociology. In this way, you're not just a guy trying to ask a woman out at a bar, you're a scientist collecting data to test your hypothesis, using the scientific method. Before you do anything, be mindful of the fact that some people just don't wish to socialize and do your best to read the situation before proceeding. It's advisable to avoid attempting to engage with someone who is evidently avoiding conversation or social interaction in general, as indicated by their lack of eye contact or their body orientation away from the crowd. Try to discern a shared interest or connection through the individual's non-verbal cues or at least begin the conversation with a topic that showcases or hints at the depth of your own character. The attention market is saturated with low-effort, half-hearted attempts at interaction, so originality and sincerity are crucial. In any case, if the approach is thoughtful and respectful, the potential for harsh consequence is low.

Begin by creating a spreadsheet to track your attempts at asking someone out. Document each attempt, noting the positive and negative responses. Incorporate columns for details

such as the location, time of day, and your approach method. Don't forget to include any other observations that might shed light on the individual's receptiveness to your advances. Now you're gathering empirical evidence to confirm or disprove the assertions made by these self-help enthusiasts who claim to have all the answers. You are the one with power because you are on a quest for knowledge, not merely accepting others' ideas in blind faith. And if you happen to secure a few dates in the process, consider that a bonus. But the real objective here is knowledge, which you will gain regardless of the momentary outcome. The data is the goal in this scenario, and the scientific method doesn't allow for embarrassment, so keep that in mind as you make your observations and apply rigorous methodology to test your hypothesis objectively. While the details of this description are centered on dating, this method is universally applicable to various social interactions, be it forging friendships or establishing business connections.

In the pursuit of knowledge through empirical evidence, it's also important to remain vigilant of the cognitive biases that may skew both our data collection and its interpretation. Biases often operate below the level of conscious awareness, subtly influencing how we perceive and react to various situations, so always take a moment to make sure you are not reading into some subtext which may be nonexistent. Be careful to avoid any sort of quick assessment which may just be the product of your own pre-conceived assumptions.

Understanding these biases not only enriches the rigor of our self-initiated sociological research but can also provide a

pivotal framework for navigating societal norms and expectations. It sets the stage for exploring how the same biases might manifest in other realms, such as professional evaluations, where experience and authority can unduly sway our judgment.

For example, when a seasoned veteran of a particular discipline suggests a notion which could be considered DIY or rough-around-the-edges, they might be praised for having ready insight that allows them to get the job done, even when all the resources aren't available. But if a novice were to make the same DIY, "cut corners" type of suggestion, it might be discarded or looked down upon as proof of the ignorance that goes along with inexperience. A clear authority bias logical fallacy (argument from authority or appeal to authority).

The difference in reaction to similar suggestions from a seasoned veteran and a novice demonstrates the powerful influence of authority bias in our decision-making processes. We place an undue emphasis on the opinions of perceived authorities, sometimes to the point of ignoring other valuable perspectives. It's crucial to remember that experience, while invaluable, doesn't equate to infallibility, and inexperience doesn't automatically discredit an individual's contribution.

What is the basis for the bias? We can trace this back to ancient civilizations, where kings and queens were considered divine or chosen by the gods, and their words became law, not merely because of their leadership qualities, but because of the reverence and authority attributed to their position. Fast-forward to modern times, and we find CEOs, influencers, and thought leaders, whose opinions are often taken as gospel.

This kind of deference to authority can lead to a blind acceptance of ideas without scrutiny. However, it's not just about the followers; those in power too, can fall victim to their own hype. They might become siloed in an ideological echo chamber, surrounded by yes-men and shielded from critical feedback, leading to decisions made without full reflection. The reciprocal nature of this bias, where one seeks guidance and the other enjoys the position of providing it, reinforces a cycle that can stifle critical thinking and independent judgment. It underscores the importance of cultivating a discerning mindset and understanding the dynamics at play, especially in a world where information and opinions are abundant.

A DIY approach or a cutting-edge idea can be equally valid and valuable, regardless of its source, as long as the claim is scrutinized, and the argument is warranted. By acknowledging this bias and deliberately seeking to challenge it, we can open up space for innovative ideas, prioritize objectivity, and move towards a more holistic understanding of the world.

Having briefly touched upon a few cognitive biases just now, it's important to enumerate some of the more common ones in greater detail, giving us a chance to understand and explore further examples of how these biases can subtly influence our daily interactions, decisions, and perceptions.

CHAPTER SEVEN

Confluence of Cognitive Biases: Shaping the Sociocultural Landscape

There exists somewhere in the range of 100 or more cognitive biases that afflict our daily thought processes. This list is by no means exhaustive, but it defines a few of the more common biases we might encounter:

Ambiguity Effect – The tendency to avoid options for which the probability of a favorable outcome is unknown. Given a choice between a stock with a known 70% chance of return and a potentially higher-yielding but uncertain stock, the ambiguity effect leads one to choose the former due to its clear probability.

Anchoring – The tendency to rely too heavily, or "anchor," on one trait or piece of information when making decisions (usually the first piece of information acquired on that subject).

Authority Bias – The tendency to attribute greater accuracy or weight to the opinions of an authority figure, even when other evidence might contradict that authority's opinion.

Example: Jane has been feeling fatigued and experiencing joint pain. After doing some research online, she believes she may have symptoms consistent with a specific autoimmune disorder. She visits her general practitioner and shares her concerns. After a brief examination, the doctor dismisses her concerns, saying it's probably just stress and recommends she take some time off work and rest more. Jane, trusting her doctor as an authority figure in health, doesn't seek a second opinion and follows the advice. Months pass, and her symptoms worsen. Finally, after seeing a specialist, she is diagnosed with the autoimmune disorder she suspected.

Jane's initial decision not to seek further advice or a second opinion, despite her symptoms and initial beliefs, is influenced by authority bias. She trusted her doctor's judgment more than her own observations and research, leading her to delay seeking a correct diagnosis and appropriate treatment.

The rise of authority bias in social media users reflects the world's increasingly divisive sociocultural climate. Historically and culturally, we're predisposed to trust figures like fathers, chieftains, or religious leaders, rarely challenging their assertions. This intrinsic trust stems from a deep-rooted desire to believe such figures have our best interests at heart, or that "might makes right" since the alpha position was usually the result of the biggest and strongest asserting dominance over the lesser males, leading us to align our identities with their

tribe or group, embracing their words as our own. Statistical models might suggest that this is biologically required behavior, as non-compliance with a singular group identity would make it difficult to organize and optimize resources effectively for survival.

Belief Bias – An effect where someone's evaluation of the logical strength of an argument is biased by the believability of the conclusion. In the realm of criminal justice, eyewitness testimony, though compelling, can sometimes be unreliable. Memory can be influenced by various factors, leading to misidentifications. Imagine a crime has been committed and the primary evidence against a suspect is an eyewitness who confidently identifies that person as the culprit. The jury hears the testimony and is presented with other evidence that, logically, casts doubt on the reliability of the eyewitness (e.g., the eyewitness had poor vision, it was dark, or they saw the suspect from a distance).

However, due to belief bias, the jury might place undue weight on the eyewitness's confident testimony because they believe in the general idea that "seeing is believing." They may think, "Why would the eyewitness lie? They sounded so sure." Consequently, they might overlook the logical inconsistency and evidence suggesting that the identification is unreliable.

This tendency to rely heavily on eyewitness testimonies, even when other evidence casts doubt, has led to wrongful convictions. Organizations like the Innocence Project have exonerated individuals based on DNA evidence, where primary convictions were heavily reliant on misidentifications by eyewitnesses. The belief bias here is the overconfidence in

human memory and the assumption that if someone believes they saw something, it must be accurate. The jury in this scenario could also be experiencing confirmation or authority bias, if the eyewitness's testimony aligns with a narrative the jury already believes to be true, they might be more inclined to accept it and dismiss conflicting evidence, or by placing undue weight on the witness testimony so they are the primary source of information.

Compassion Fade – The predisposition to behave more compassionately towards a small number of identifiable victims than to a large number of anonymous ones.

Confirmation Bias – Tendency to search for or interpret information in a way that confirms one's preconceptions and discredits information that does not support the initial opinion.

Cryptomnesia – A form of misattribution where a memory is mistaken for imagination because there is no subjective experience of it being a memory.

Denomination Effect – The tendency to spend more money when it is denominated in small amounts (e.g., coins) rather than large amounts (e.g., bills). Buying a $1 item might feel more justifiable when using coins, but might seem less worthwhile if it means breaking a $50 bill.

Dunning-Kruger Effect – The tendency for unskilled individuals to overestimate their own ability and the tendency for experts to underestimate their own ability. Consider the realm of social media, where platforms like Twitter (X), Tik-Tok, and YouTube allow for instant dissemination of

opinions, and the proliferation of commentary among the general public:

Example: Alex recently read a few articles on a political issue and watched a couple of documentaries on YouTube. Feeling informed, he starts tweeting his opinions, presenting them as definitive facts. His posts, being assertive and simplistic, gain traction among those who are similarly uninformed or seeking easy-to-digest viewpoints. Emboldened by the retweets and likes, Alex starts to see himself as a knowledgeable commentator on a wide range of issues, even though his understanding is superficial.

Samantha has a degree in political science and has spent years studying various socio-political issues. She is well-aware of the complexities and nuances involved. When she shares her analyses on social media, she often uses qualifiers like "possibly," "might," or "from one perspective," understanding that few issues are black and white. Her posts, while more accurate, might be perceived as less confident or less engaging to the average reader compared to Alex's.

As the number of likes, shares, and comments grow on Alex's posts, he becomes more convinced of his expertise, not realizing that popularity on social media does not equate to accuracy or depth of understanding. Meanwhile, Samantha might begin to feel that she doesn't understand the issues as well as she thought, simply because her more nuanced takes don't receive as much attention or validation as Alex's more simplistic views.

At the heart of the Dunning-Kruger effect is the idea that those with limited knowledge or skill in a particular domain

often lack the metacognitive ability to recognize their deficits. In simpler terms, you need a certain level of skill or knowledge to accurately evaluate that skill or knowledge. If Socrates were alive today, he would likely concur, though he might view the contemporary cultural scene with profound dismay.

Sometimes, the Dunning-Krueger effect gives way to authority bias when individuals lean heavily on their credentials, using them as their main instrument to counter opposing views, rather than presenting well-reasoned arguments or analyses, and often interpreting data through their own biased lens. There are a few potential causes for this. As proposed by psychologist Carol Dweck, a fixed mindset (believing that abilities are static and unchangeable) can make individuals more susceptible to both biases. Experts with a fixed mindset might resist feedback and rely on their authority more. If the exposure to new information results in a state of discomfort due to cognitive dissonance, the expert might double down on the preconceived notions or information as an ego survival reflex. The situation is made even worse if the expert is surrounded by those who hold monolithic beliefs and are themselves resistant to conflicting ideas, creating an echo chamber where critical feedback is dismissed.

False Memory – A form of misattribution where imagination is mistaken for a memory.

Hindsight Bias – Sometimes called the "I-knew-it-all-along" effect, the tendency to see past events as being predictable at the time those events happened.

Hyperbolic Discounting – The tendency for people to have a stronger preference for more immediate payoffs

relative to later payoffs. Hyperbolic discounting leads to choices that are inconsistent over time—people make decisions today that their future selves would prefer not to have made, despite using the same reasoning. Also known as current moment bias, present-bias, and related to dynamic inconsistency. A good example of this: a study showed that when making food choices for the coming week, 74% of participants chose fruit, whereas when the food choice was for the current day, 70% chose chocolate. This bias can also be discerned when comparing the mindsets of entrepreneurs and wage workers. Entrepreneurs often display a greater willingness to embrace delayed gratification and endure short-term setbacks in hopes of future gains. In contrast, wage workers typically seek immediate compensation, proportionally aligned with their immediate effort.

Illusion of Asymmetric Insight – People perceive their knowledge of their peers to surpass their peers' knowledge of them, e.g., feeling that our inner complexity is less visible than our peers'.

Illusion of Control – The tendency to overestimate one's degree of influence over other external events.

Example: Sarah frequently plays the lottery. Instead of opting for a computer-generated "quick pick" number, she chooses her own numbers each time. She often uses significant dates like birthdays, anniversaries, or numbers she believes to be "lucky" due to past experiences. Even though the lottery is a random event, and each number combination has an equal chance of being drawn, Sarah believes that by picking her own numbers, she has a higher chance of winning

compared to someone who lets the computer choose for them. She feels that her personal strategy gives her some measure of control over a completely unpredictable outcome. In reality, Sarah's chosen numbers don't increase her odds of winning compared to any other combination. Her belief that her personal system or strategy gives her an edge is an example of the illusion of control bias.

The bias often surfaces in subtle ways, rooted in the same underlying misconception. In the film industry, a producer is tasked with ensuring that a movie is delivered on time, within budget, and meets a certain quality standard. This involves coordinating staff, vendors, schedules, budget allocation, and more. However, when unexpected issues arise—be it due to unpredictable weather, equipment malfunction, or last-minute location obstacles (e.g., location owner showing up late, preventing crew access to the set, causing schedule delays)—the producer is still held accountable for resolution, despite these elements being outside their control. Perfect foresight is an unrealistic expectation, yet many seem to believe that a producer should have this almost magical ability to anticipate every potential challenge. This is a case where external parties impose an unfair expectation of control onto an individual—a subtle but clear manifestation of the illusion of control bias towards others.

Impact Bias – The tendency to overestimate the length or the intensity of the impact of future feeling states.

Example: Jack has been working at the same company for several years and is eagerly waiting for a promotion. He

believes that if he gets the promotion, he will be overwhelmingly happy, and if he doesn't, he will be devastated for months.

Outcome 1 (Overestimation of Positive Emotion): Jack gets the promotion. He's ecstatic for a few days, feeling a mix of pride and happiness. However, after a couple of weeks, the novelty wears off. The daily tasks and responsibilities of the job set in, and while he's pleased with his advancement, the intense joy he felt initially fades much quicker than he had anticipated.

Outcome 2 (Overestimation of Negative Emotion): Jack doesn't get the promotion. He's disappointed and sad for a few days, questioning his worth and capabilities. However, within a couple of weeks, he finds himself adapting to the situation. He might even discover new opportunities or challenges in his current position that reignite his passion. His devastation doesn't last nearly as long as he feared. In both outcomes, Jack overestimated the length and intensity of his emotional reactions.

Ingroup Bias – The tendency for people to give preferential treatment to others they perceive to be members of their own groups.

Example: Two high schools, Riverdale High and Lakeside High, have a fierce rivalry, especially in basketball. Anna is a student at Riverdale High. She attends every basketball game and is a big supporter of her school's team. One day, she watches a game where a player from Riverdale and a player from Lakeside both make similar aggressive moves during the game. When discussing the game with her friends later, Anna

mentions how skillful and strategic the Riverdale player's move was, highlighting his talent and quick thinking. However, when referring to the Lakeside player's identical move, she labels it as "dirty play" and "unsportsmanlike." In this scenario, Anna's perception and interpretation of the exact same action changes based on the group membership of the player. She views the action of the Riverdale player (her ingroup) in a positive light and the action of the Lakeside player (the outgroup) in a negative light. This illustrates ingroup bias.

Irrational Escalation – The phenomenon where people justify increased investment in a decision, based on the cumulative prior investment, despite new evidence suggesting that the decision was probably wrong. Also known as the sunk cost fallacy.

Misinformation Effect – Memory becoming less accurate because of interference from post-event information.

Example: Two cars collide at an intersection. You witness the accident, and from your perspective, both cars were going at roughly the same speed before the crash. A few days later, you're discussing the accident with a friend. Your friend says, "I heard one of the cars was speeding really fast right before the accident." A week after that, you're asked by the police to provide a statement about what you saw. Even though, on the day of the accident, you thought both cars were going at roughly the same speed, the comment from your friend has influenced your memory. Now, you're not entirely sure anymore, and you report to the police that one of the cars might have been speeding before the collision. Your memory of the event has been distorted by the post-event information (your

friend's comment), even though it wasn't part of the original event. This is an example of the misinformation effect in action.

Selection Bias – When the members of a statistical sample are not chosen completely at random, which leads to the sample not being representative of the population. An intriguing parallel can be drawn from Apple's decision to adjust the shuffle feature on their music app. Users reported instances where they'd hear multiple songs from the same album consecutively, which felt less random due to the patterns they perceived. In response, Apple tweaked the algorithm to make the shuffle feel more random to users, even though true randomness can naturally result in such sequences. It's a manifestation of the human tendency to seek patterns, even when dealing with genuinely random processes.

Survivorship Bias – Concentrating on the people or things that "survived" some process and inadvertently overlooking those that didn't because of their lack of visibility. This dynamic is also true of the inverse, where we focus more on the numerous misfortunes presented before us, without considering the possibility that it wasn't a complete wash for all members of the particular group in question.

Naïve Realism – The belief that we see reality as it really is—objectively and without bias; that the facts are plain for all to see; that rational people will agree with us; and that those who don't are uninformed, lazy, irrational, or biased.

Puritanical Bias – Refers to the tendency to attribute cause of an undesirable outcome or wrongdoing by an individual to

a moral deficiency or lack of self-control rather than considering the impact of broader societal determinants.

Reactance – The urge to do the opposite of what someone wants you to do out of a need to resist a perceived attempt to constrain your freedom of choice.

Naïve realism, puritanical bias, and psychological reactance intermingle in modern society, forming a dynamic heuristic model that profoundly shapes and reflects cultural currents. These phenomena, deeply ingrained in human cognition and behavior, have been extensively studied by psychologists and sociologists alike (Ross & Ward, 1996; Miller & Ratner, 1998; Brehm, 1966).

The concept of naïve realism—the conviction that we perceive the world exactly as it exists—can inadvertently deepen societal rifts. This is because it becomes difficult for individuals grounded in this belief to understand or validate the diverse perspectives and interpretations of their peers. Parallelly, puritanical bias echoes society's esteem for discipline and diligence, prescribing stringent behavioral norms. This often stands at odds with the increasingly prevalent cultural pivot towards championing individual rights and freedoms.

Jack Brehm's theory of psychological reactance offers another layer to this analysis. It suggests that when people perceive threats to their freedoms, they double down, advocating more fervently for their rights. This pushback is particularly notable today, in an era where the autonomy of personal choices and self-expression holds significant cultural weight.

Juxtaposing these principles unveils the inherent dichotomies shaping modern culture. We find ourselves caught between venerating traditional puritan values of hard work and restraint, and a growing emphasis on celebrating individual uniqueness. The tension between these ideals, intensified by puritanical biases and the challenges of naïve realism, manifests in a society rife with mixed signals and inconsistent expectations. Such a dynamic underscores the multifaceted, intricate nature of today's cultural milieu.

CHAPTER EIGHT

Unleashing the Potency of Delusion and Belief: An Undeniable Force

Joshua Abraham Norton's life serves as a fascinating testament to the extraordinary power of belief. An English-born businessman and eventual resident of San Francisco, CA, Norton proclaimed himself the Emperor of the United States in 1859. Despite having previously experienced financial ruin, he rebuilt his life around this audacious claim, demonstrating the transformative power of self-belief.

Norton's self-proclamation, bold and unconventional as it was, reflected an exceptional ability to reimagine himself. Amid the harsh realities of his working-class life, he chose to construct a new identity, effectively turning the tables on his circumstances. The San Francisco community exhibited a collective willingness to play along with Norton's delusions, recognizing the harmless joy and unity it brought to their diverse city. When his uniform began to wear out, the city's Board of

Supervisors even bought him a suitably imperial replacement. Newspapers found Norton to be an intriguing character and frequently published his imperial "decrees." The constant coverage only solidified his presence and acceptance in the local Bay Area, and seemed to endear him towards the residents. He even issued his own currency, which local businesses and community members accepted, more out of amusement or respect for him than any actual belief in its value. This wasn't exactly charity though, as restaurants he dined at would advertise his patronage to attract customers. The community quickly recognized that embracing Norton's harmless eccentricity could be profitable, so a bit of grandiose delusion morphed into a symbiotic relationship with said community.

This imaginative leap, fueled by an unshakable belief in himself, shaped Norton's life in profound ways. He is rumored to have corresponded with figures like King Kamehameha V of Hawaii and possibly even Queen Victoria, despite lacking any official political standing. While the veracity of these interactions remains uncertain, they contribute to the aura of legitimacy and the colorful lore that surrounded Emperor Norton, further embellishing his self-styled position of importance. His story illuminates how the power of belief, or even delusion, can influence our actions, shape our interactions, and affect our reality. It serves as a particularly profound lesson for many of us, since it almost immediately and instinctively violates every conditioned, conventional wisdom trope we have come to believe and embrace in society. It may even trigger a degree of bitter hostility towards the man, for essentially doing what so many of us wish we could do: say "fuck you" to the shackles of societal conformity and do things our

own way. Although, it certainly didn't seem like Norton had such reactionary or counterculture motivations, as he was known to be gentlemanly to those he encountered within the community and abroad. And perhaps that is the key foundational principle to understand here. You don't earn respect purely by asserting yourself as the "alpha," you achieve it through sincerity and practical kindness.

Now, this isn't to suggest that we should delude ourselves or adopt grandiose self-proclamations, devoid of rational self-assessment. Rather, it's to emphasize the transformative power of belief in shaping our lives. By cultivating a strong, positive self-belief, and sincere display of kindness to those around us, we can influence our circumstances, overcome setbacks, and create our own unique path. Norton's life serves as a reminder that the stories we tell ourselves about who we are and what we're capable of can have profound effects on our reality.

The Paradox of Narcissism: Confidence, Competence, and Innate Abilities

The tale of Josh Norton showcases the uplifting power of belief, illustrating how positive self-assessment can yield benefits not just for the individual, but for the wider community as well. Yet, in stark contrast, it also hints at a more ominous flip side to the narrative of self-affirmation: the dangerous descent into narcissism.

Narcissism paints an intriguing paradox: the audacious confidence of narcissists often masks a hollow center, devoid of the competence they project. Their self-assured demeanor, coupled with charisma, can beguile those around them, yet when faced with tasks demanding true proficiency, their skills often fall short (Paulhus, D. L. 1998). This paradox might help us understand a broader spectrum of human behavior, as it extends far beyond the clinical definitions of narcissism and taps into our very nature as social animals.

In the animal kingdom, innate competence, the inherent ability to survive and reproduce, takes precedence over all else. Predators don't need to convince their prey of their prowess; they simply demonstrate it. Similarly, a bird doesn't boast about its ability to build a nest; it just does so. For animals, survival doesn't depend on the illusion of competence but rather the unvarnished reality of it.

Humans, too, carry innate competence within them, though our complex societies often limit opportunities for this intrinsic proficiency to emerge. Our built environment, for instance, seldom demands the level of physical exertion, awareness, and adaptability our ancestors required to survive. Yet these latent abilities remain within us, ready to be awakened when necessary.

Narcissists, curiously, seem to exploit this disparity. They create an illusion of competence, substituting our innate, often dormant abilities with an amplified display of confidence. Their survival mechanism doesn't involve direct confrontation with physical realities, but instead navigates social landscapes, using charisma and perceived competence to gain influence and control (Twenge and Campbell, 2009). Alternatively, they may lack any semblance of charisma but compensate by displaying aggression or arrogance. This behavior is reminiscent of an animal asserting dominance despite not possessing the quintessential quiet confidence of a true leader. It leads us to a fascinating examination of the concept of the "beta male," which we will explore later. This archetype often embodies traits that, paradoxically, are antisocial and counterproductive, yet sometimes pass for signs of success.

When navigating situations with potential narcissists, it's essential to tread carefully. We don't want to throw clinical terminology around haphazardly, as any official diagnosis should be reserved for professionals, so it's best not to jump to conclusions. However, if you have reasons to suspect narcissistic tendencies, there are methods to handle the situation gracefully. The Paulhus study highlights that the seemingly robust confidence of a narcissist can unravel over time, without any outside push. This happens because, beneath their bravado, narcissists often grapple with deep-seated insecurities and shame. By closely observing their behavior over several interactions, you can discern patterns and see the façade give way. Another strategy is a gentle probe or question about their claims. Often, this is enough to make their constructed image waver, revealing the reality beneath.

This analysis offers insight into the complexities of human behavior and how it has evolved from its original survival-driven form. The narcissist's confidence, unmoored from genuine competence, is a peculiar outgrowth of our sociocultural evolution. Unmasking this illusion can prompt us to better understand and value innate competence, placing authenticity and ability at the heart of our esteem for others and ourselves.

PART THREE

Understanding Goals and Personal Achievement

Probing the Heart of Our Ambitions: The Crucial Analysis of Our Goals and Strategies

The physical realm offers us a tangible understanding of effort and reward, more in line with our intrinsic animal nature. The harder we push, the more we train, the more apparent our progress becomes. This tangibility fosters a clear correlation between effort and reward, conditioning us to value hard work and perseverance. In contrast, the abstract realm, which includes ideas, creativity, and personal growth, doesn't always adhere to the same linear correlation. This isn't to say that effort isn't necessary or beneficial. Still, the process of "working harder" becomes nebulous and often misleading when applied to abstract endeavors.

Let's consider the process of generating creative ideas or developing personal skills. Here, the concept of "working harder" can take on a different meaning. It might involve fostering curiosity, cultivating diverse experiences, or even

allowing periods of rest and reflection, activities that may seem contrary to the conventional wisdom of "hard work." The same applies to navigating personal growth or effecting behavioral change; self-compassion, patience, and introspection might be more beneficial than sheer effort. Adding to this, we must also contend with the fluctuating parameters of societal expectations. As we seek success within the abstract realm, we are invariably influenced by the prevailing cultural standards and norms. This could mean that despite our hard work and progress, we may find ourselves "out of step" with the current zeitgeist or societal values. Therefore, it becomes critical to understand and accept the inherent differences between the physical and abstract realms. One is not superior to the other, but each requires a unique set of strategies and approaches. In the abstract realm, it's often more about "working smarter" rather than "working harder." This could mean refining our approach, seeking diverse perspectives, fostering resilience, and embracing adaptability.

Individuals raised in families with deep-rooted conservative values might recognize this contrast between the abstract nature of purpose and the literal interpretation of what must be done. The essence of traditional thinking often harkens back to simpler times when life had fewer complexities that clouded one's sense of purpose. Historically, people often chose the most straightforward path and made the best of it. Much of our conflict in society today comes from the reconciliation of these realities.

As we navigate the abstract realm, it is important to remember that our individual journeys are uniquely ours.

Success and progress are often subjective and not always aligned with societal expectations. It's crucial to define our parameters for success and to be open to the continuous evolution of our ideas, creativity, and personal growth. It's a challenging yet rewarding journey, reflective of the complexity and richness of the human experience.

When we try to apply effort to improve an abstract situation, we are liable to overlook and exclude details that are beyond our control. How does someone become a more "likable" person, without conforming to behaviors that seem disingenuous? If we strive to connect with people, but genuinely couldn't care less about them. What is the method for overcoming this apathetic disposition? There are all sorts of theories and methods that practitioners try to shill, but the bottom line could simply be that you are not meant to occupy this singular ecosystem of individuals. Let's say you go to therapy and "do the work" to try to resolve childhood traumas and neurotic maladaptation, in order to form better interpersonal connections: our cognitive biases compel us to believe that the only reason it wouldn't work with certainty, is because we were not trying hard enough, or it just wasn't the right method for us. But that argument has notes of a gambler's justification to it. "Well, you just got to keep trying until you win!" "Maybe blackjack is the game for you, not poker." And if you lived your life in that fashion, it's very likely you will end up broke and hopeless when the act of continuously trying doesn't yield positive results. Maybe you just don't belong in a casino. And maybe you just don't belong in whatever system you are desperately trying to fit yourself within.

By no stretch of the imagination, life has a way of resembling a random game of chance, with our destiny seemingly dictated by rolls of dice. Yet, there are moments when our expectations and reality seem woefully out of sync, making life feel as though we're attempting to win the California state lottery while we're rolling dice at a casino table in Las Vegas. We find ourselves pinned between disparate dimensions: the wide-ranging hope of a windfall from the lottery and the limited, immediate outcomes of a dice game. The desired outcome appears detached from the actual circumstances we find ourselves in, highlighting our disconnect with reality. This misalignment can lead to confusion and frustration, as we strive for goals that seem unattainable within our current frame of reference.

The key to bridging this gap may lie in adjusting our expectations, reevaluating our goals, and aligning them more closely with our actual circumstances. It's about understanding the game we're actually playing, not the one we wish we were. In this way, we can navigate our path more effectively, making strategic decisions based on the actual options available to us rather than chasing distant, incongruent dreams. This approach can help ground our experience in reality, empowering us to make progress within the bounds of our current situation, while still keeping an eye on the broader horizons of our aspirations.

This inherent tendency to follow a predetermined narrative path is a common pattern among humans. We can find it hard to recognize when our efforts to fit in are actually contributing to our discomfort or dissatisfaction. A crucial, often

neglected part of our self-improvement journey is understanding the systems we are engaging with and recognizing when they are fundamentally incompatible with our authentic selves.

As per the metaphor in our earlier discussion, consider the example of the casino. In this instance, the casino serves as a symbol for societal expectations and norms. It's easy to believe that if we're not winning at the games presented to us—if we're not succeeding according to these norms—then we must be doing something wrong. We need to try harder, adjust our strategies, or perhaps change the game we're playing. However, these "solutions" imply that the problem lies within us rather than in the larger system we're interacting with. This narrative is overly simplified and fails to account for the complexities of human behavior, psychology, and societal influences. It fails to question the legitimacy of the casino itself, the fairness of the games, and whether it even suits us to be a part of this ecosystem.

While some individuals may thrive within the established parameters of the "casino," others may find these norms oppressive, restrictive, or otherwise unsuitable to their needs and values. This doesn't mean that those who don't fit in are in some way deficient or flawed—it simply indicates a mismatch between the individual and the system. We need to move away from a one-size-fits-all approach to social integration and start accepting the diversity of the human experience. Instead of aiming to conform to existing models, we should focus on exploring and understanding our authentic selves, learning how to create an environment where we can flourish as individuals.

If we find ourselves continuously struggling in the "casino," the solution may not be to keep gambling but rather to find a different venue entirely. This is not to advocate for isolation, but instead for the pursuit of a more authentic form of connection, an ecosystem that resonates with our unique attributes and perspectives. It might take more effort to find or create this kind of environment, but the resulting sense of belonging and fulfillment can be transformative.

The key takeaway here is that our worth is not determined by how well we fit into a specific societal structure or by how successful we are according to established norms. Self-improvement is not about becoming more likable or socially acceptable; it's about becoming more in tune with our authentic selves and finding a community where this authenticity is celebrated rather than suppressed or exploited.

Therefore, the next time you find yourself desperately trying to win at a game that doesn't suit you, remember that maybe you just don't belong in that particular casino, and perhaps it's advisable that you leave Vegas altogether. It's time to take a step back, reassess, and look for an environment where you can truly thrive, and hopefully head out the door while you still have some money in your bank account.

CHAPTER ELEVEN

Alchemical Success: The Influence of Personal Aura

While the prior analogy warns of the perils of remaining in situations where the self is in discord with the environment, exemplary figures like Steve Lafferty showcase the alchemical prowess to transform any circumstance into proverbial gold.

Steve's metaphorical representation within the entertainment industry as a "whale among sharks" underscores an important principle of successful leadership: the potency of personal presence. While the "sharks" engage in a relentless struggle for dominance, partaking in the feeding frenzy trope, the "whale" thrives not by competing, but by confidently occupying its rightful space within the ecosystem. This serene confidence, coupled with a magnanimous nature, defines the essence of individuals like Steve, setting them apart in the sea of competition.

Steve Lafferty joined Creative Artists Agency in 1990 and later ascended to lead the agency's television department.

Prior to that, he was the Executive Vice President at the literary and talent agency, Triad. Lafferty has a rich background in the entertainment industry, having served as Vice President of Business Affairs at Showtime Entertainment and holding various management roles at Viacom-owned entities such as The Movie Channel and Viacom Productions. He graduated from Whittier Law School in 1978 and, during his studies, worked at MTM Enterprises. Lafferty completed his undergraduate studies at the University of California, Santa Barbara in 1975, earning a degree in psychology and philosophy. (https://variety.com/exec/steve-lafferty/)

Success, as exemplified by Steve, transcends conventional markers, such as accolades or skills. While these attributes are essential, they aren't necessarily the defining elements that leave an indelible imprint on our consciousness. Instead, it's often the person's aura, the tangible yet intangible "vibe" they exude, that leaves a lasting impression. Having only crossed paths with Steve a handful of times, it's undeniable that there's a captivating magnetism about him, which is challenging to describe in relatable terms unless you've personally felt it. Even as I write these words, I acknowledge that it could be an exercise in futility to articulate this abstract. However, this is the energetic essence that shapes our perception and experience of a person. Individuals like Steve do more than merely capitalize on favorable circumstances. They embody a form of success alchemy, transforming each moment and situation into an opportunity. Their mere presence influences their surroundings, subtly shifting the dynamics in their favor. They become the "right time and place," creating a ripple effect that

transforms their environment and sets the stage for their success.

By studying and embodying these characteristics, we can learn to cultivate our own unique, magnetic presence, transforming our interactions and experiences in profound ways. This is the true art of success alchemy: not merely adapting to the world, but inspiring the world to adapt to us, allowing us to manifest our highest potential.

CHAPTER TWELVE

Outcome vs. Process Orientations

Having delved into the profound impact of personal aura and its transformative power in the realm of success, it's essential to also understand how individual orientations shape our interactions and understanding of the world around us. A prominent example of this distinction can be observed in the contrasting ways genders approach situations.

Men are from Mars, Women are from Venus, by John Gray, is a widely recognized book that explores gender differences in communication styles, emotional needs, and modes of behavior. According to Gray, men and women are as different as beings from other planets, leading to inevitable misunderstandings and conflicts. He emphasizes how understanding and respecting these differences can improve relationships.

From a sociological perspective, it's evident that genders often differ in their approach based on outcome or process-

oriented thinking. Men generally lean towards object or out-come-driven thought, emphasizing efficiency, problem-solving, and directness. In contrast, women predominantly adopt a person or process-oriented mindset, prioritizing the journey itself and claiming to value empathy, inclusivity, and sensitivity to group dynamics. This isn't merely a preference, but often serves as a key source of validation in their interactions. We'll explore this notion of the outcome vs. process orientation from a few other angles later in the book.

In Gray's analogy, men (Mars) are depicted as autonomous, goal-oriented individuals (outcome-focused), whereas women (Venus) are seen as relational and emotionally expressive beings (process-oriented). While this perspective has been critiqued for its broad generalizations and the potential to reinforce harmful stereotypes, it does echo the outcome vs. process distinction in some ways. It's important to note that these models are not absolute or universally applicable. Both men and women can exhibit a mix of outcome-oriented and process-oriented thinking, influenced by factors such as individual personality, cultural context, and personal experiences. The utility of these models lies in their ability to provide a starting point for understanding and communication, not in boxing individuals into predefined categories.

In the realm of relationships, many men recognize this difference in process versus outcome orientation between genders, even if they've never framed it that way. Speaking from my own experience, I remember multiple disagreements with female companions where I aimed to find a solution, while my partner or peer seemed more inclined to reflect on the issue,

was acutely aware of the potential repercussions a decision might have on group dynamics or her standing within said group, even if the decision that maintained balance within the group led to greater distress or sacrifice on her part, when alternative action could have effectively solved the issue for everyone.

I recall one instance when a friend of mine had scheduled time off from work for a vacation trip, which had been pre-approved by her boss. However, a week before the break, a colleague revealed to her in private that he was leaving the company. This surprise exit was out of spite and timed right when the firm was busiest. His departure meant the team would be without crucial managerial support, potentially harming the remaining staff and the boss, who'd be short of key personnel. While my friend disliked working for this supervisor, she considered sacrificing her vacation to assist, even though she had acted responsibly, and her colleague had not. I suggested she inform the boss about his sudden departure to find an alternative solution. But she hesitated, fearing it would cause group tension by outing her as the informant, despite the fact he was leaving anyway, and the superior would actually prefer to know this information ahead of time. She was ready to compromise her peace of mind to avoid possible discord—a clear demonstration of prioritizing process and group harmony over a proactive outcome that squares practicality with virtue and well-being.

On another occasion, a partner confided in me that she had been abused by a previous boyfriend. I was deeply disturbed by this revelation. Her ex was quite successful, and she

held him in high regard, so she was less inclined to do anything which might jeopardize a potential professional relationship or future opportunity. When I proposed she report the incident or take other action, she viewed my reaction as excessive. However, when he gained more media attention years later as a result of his growing career and started licensing his likeness to merchandise, she chose that moment to publicly share her traumatic experience via social media, suggesting she might have been influenced by the timing to maximize the impact of her disclosure and benefit from the attention it brought her way.

In these situations, and others, I was consistently seeking a direct and justified response to address the issue presented to me, while my counterparts seemed more concerned with potential social or personal repercussions. The irony in the second scenario is that many within her circle perceived her public revelation as a mere ploy for attention, leading to further criticism. But as the saying goes, "any publicity is good publicity" and this is certainly true for men and women who possess the process validation mindset.

While the tendencies I described earlier often align with gender, there are exceptions, as is typical with any population's normal distribution. I've certainly had moments that deviated from the logical outcome approach.

Several years ago, I crossed paths with someone in an unexpected place: waiting in line at LAX. The randomness of our meeting, almost like a scene from a romance movie, was a story I'd often retell. At first, we'd meet for coffee sporadically, maybe once every few months, but eventually an invite

to the Magic Castle deepened our connection. Our initial bond was strong and almost surreal, leaving an impression that I still vividly recall. However, as time went on, the harmony we first felt began to waver—as is so often the case with volatile personality types—and she expressed doubts about our compatibility. Wanting to avoid any pressure, I suggested we just go with the flow, since we still enjoyed each other's company. Well, a billion or so other men can probably relate to that point of view and understand exactly how it usually turns out. On paper, the rational outcome-oriented mind would deem us compatible if graded against a conventional societal rubric, conveniently sidelining the evident disparities in our personalities. She held a mirrored perspective, albeit driven by different societal pressures, trapping us in a repetitive rotation, influenced by life's unpredictable ebb and flow. The resulting dynamic felt like an endless cycle of polarity shifts, a perpetual push and pull, reminiscent of a disengaged electric motor armature.

After a draining year and a half of this exhausting process, common sense prevailed, and we finally decided to part ways for good. Despite seeing myself as a logical and astute individual, I had to accept that I made grave errors, ones I'd have instantly cautioned others against if I were an outside observer. So why did it happen? I was stuck in the process of thinking this person reflects so well upon me, and she hits all the conventional metrics for a qualitatively "ideal" partner. I was tangled up in the mess of social acceptance, but hell, I know plenty of men who've tumbled down that same rabbit hole. A beautiful woman will make a man stupid, causing him to toss caution to the wind, blind to every warning that's

waved in front of him. John Gray might assess that this acceptance could be perceived as a particular type of outcome, though he would agree that it is divorced from reality, in the sense that it is generally never sustainable. If two people can't enjoy the uninteresting and unexceptional moments together, that dynamic will likely not result in long-term happiness.

Don't get trapped in that relentless cycle. Deep down, we can sense when we're just chasing that next fleeting high, the brain's quick fix. Maybe that's all there is for some, or just what the moment demands. But over time, it'll weigh you down, making it harder to find a genuine connection. The ego's an insatiable beast, always pushing for more—a new thrill, a fresh taste. The sooner we recognize this hunger, the better. True peace comes from blending the journey and the destination, the process and the outcome. The dream must align with shared values, and you've got to find comfort in the simple moments. Maybe you can't find that with everyone, given insurmountable differences. But knowing it helps in making choices that lead to greener pastures.

CHAPTER THIRTEEN

The Role of Structure in Self-Actualization and Happiness

Bridging the insights on gendered orientations, it becomes even more evident that our interactions, reactions, and choices are deeply rooted in complex sociocultural frameworks. This intricate matrix not only defines our views on gender roles and interpersonal dynamics but also extends to broader aspects of our identity and aspirations. In understanding this foundation, we pave the way for delving deeper into the role of structure in our personal journeys of self-actualization and happiness. As we transition, we'll see how established theories further elucidate our internal and external worlds.

A three-tier model of conceptualization can be illuminated using theories from both sociological and philosophical schools of thought. There are several domains where these theories intersect, and they offer us ways to better understand and explore this model.

1. That which we are unaware of: The sociological and philosophical underpinnings here might best be reflected in the work of Pierre Bourdieu and his concept of "habitus." Habitus refers to the deep-seated, often unconscious, habits, skills, and dispositions that we've acquired through our life experiences and social conditioning. We're generally unaware of our habitus, yet it shapes our perceptions, attitudes, and behaviors. From a philosophical point of view, this is akin to Kant's concept of "noumena," which refers to things as they are in themselves, independent of our perception or knowledge of them.

2. That which we perceive to know: Here, we delve into the realm of phenomenology, a school of philosophy that focuses on consciousness and the objects of direct experience. Alfred Schutz, a sociologist heavily influenced by phenomenology, posited that our understanding of the world and social action is based on the common-sense knowledge we acquire and share as members of society. In a similar vein, Karl Mannheim's sociology of knowledge examines how our societal position influences what and how we perceive to know.

3. That which we act upon: This draws heavily from the American pragmatist tradition, especially in the works of John Dewey, who argued that knowledge is primarily a tool for solving the problems we encounter in our environment. In sociology, this resonates with the ideas of symbolic interactionism, which posits that our behaviors are based on the meanings we assign to things in our environment. Moreover, sociologist Anthony Giddens' structuration theory underlines this concept, arguing that individuals' actions, based on their

knowledge, continually shape and reshape the social structures within which they operate.

These three tiers of conceptualization offer a multifaceted approach to understanding the human interaction with knowledge and the world. Recognizing these layers can help us understand the complexity of human behavior, societal structures, and our own perception of reality.

If we further analyze this this three-tiered model of conceptualization, it becomes apparent that human interactions with knowledge and the world are not isolated occurrences. Instead, they exist within and contribute to an ever-evolving cycle of structures. Just as a structure, be it societal norms or cultural practices, shapes our perceptions and actions, our individual and collective interactions reciprocally influence and mold these structures. This iterative relationship between knowledge and structure presents a compelling dance between the intangible and tangible, theory and praxis.

The notion of "structure begetting structure" finds its roots in this dynamic, along with several of the concepts we've already discussed so far. As we move from the unknown realities to perceived knowledge and ultimately to actioned knowledge, we inadvertently craft, refine, and reinforce societal structures. These structures, once established, serve as the foundation upon which future perceptions, behaviors, and systems are built. They form the scaffolding that guides societal evolution. In essence, as individuals and societies engage in the continuous process of conceptualization, they are not merely passive observers but active architects, ensuring that

structures give birth to successive generations of structures, each echoing the learnings and experiences of its predecessor.

Drawing from the three-tiered model of conceptualization, it becomes evident that our perceptions, knowledge, and actions are intertwined with the structures around us. As these structures influence and are influenced by us, they shape our journey toward personal fulfillment. Each layer of understanding and interaction either aids or hinders our alignment with our deeper values and aspirations. Recognizing, establishing, and navigating these structures empowers us to craft a life that resonates with our authentic selves, thereby leading to true personal fulfillment.

These foundational structures could range from daily routines and rituals, professional commitments, to maintaining healthy relationships. All of these, when viewed holistically, contribute to the larger overarching architecture of our existence, and ultimately, our happiness. Akin to how an architect gradually constructs a building starting from a cornerstone, we too can methodically build our lives, adding rooms of experiences, floors of knowledge, and windows of perspectives.

In the realm of the collective consciousness, a commonly held belief equates freedom to happiness, serving as a counterpoint to the formalized concept of structure we just discussed. While freedom is indeed a crucial component of personal fulfillment, the narrative often leans towards an oversimplified version of it—an image of unbridled liberty with no boundaries or obligations. This idea is frequently promoted by those who feel disenfranchised or disillusioned by their

existing circumstances, seeking an escape from perceived constraints.

However, this conceptualization of absolute freedom can lead to an aimless drift through life, lacking direction and purpose. It tends to overlook the fact that certain forms of structure can actually enhance our freedom by providing a framework within which to explore our potential and actualize our aspirations. For instance, the structure of an education system, while having boundaries, provides the freedom to learn, grow, and forge a path for future endeavors. In light of this, it is essential to strike a balance between freedom and structure. Overemphasizing one at the expense of the other can lead to either a stifling rigidity or a disorienting aimlessness. A fulfilling life requires a symbiotic relationship between freedom and structure. This interplay gives rise to opportunities to explore and realize our potential while ensuring we stay grounded and focused.

Thus, it is through the iterative process of building, maintaining, and refining structures in our lives that we can effectively navigate the challenges that come our way and ultimately cultivate a meaningful existence. As the saying goes, "Happiness is not a destination but a journey." By constructing a well-balanced structure for our journey, we are not just wandering aimlessly, but moving forward with purpose and direction, leading us towards a path of self-actualization and happiness.

As something of a cautionary counterpoint, there is another bit of modern philosophical rhetoric to address. Specifically, the misconception that visualization equates to

actionable reality—often reinforced by popular self-help doctrines and motivational mantras. While having a vision is undoubtedly crucial as a starting point for any endeavor, it is equally important to recognize the chasm that can exist between conception and realization. This gap can be bridged by tangible resources, skill sets, environmental factors, and even sheer luck. But make no mistake, the ambition must square with the precepts of reality.

For instance, one might vividly imagine and even design a car that can travel faster than the speed of light. This visual conceptualization, while inspiring, immediately clashes with Einstein's theory of relativity, which posits that nothing can move faster than light in a vacuum. Here, the laws of physics serve as a natural limitation, ensuring that the imaginative concept remains confined to the realm of science fiction.

Similarly, in the world of entrepreneurship, many startups are founded on visionary ideas. Yet, according to the Bureau of Labor (https://www.bls.gov/bdm/us_age_naics_00_table7.txt), 50% of all startups fail within their first five years. Of the data collected by CB Insights, the top reasons for these failures seem to be a lack of market demand, cash-flow issues, or simply being outcompeted. These obstacles highlight the rift between an entrepreneur's vision and the marketplace's reality, demonstrating that without proper research, planning, and resources, even the most vivid conceptualizations can fall flat.

From a sociological perspective, promoting the idea that anything is achievable through sheer will and vision can be potentially damaging. While optimism and encouragement are

vital, setting unrealistic expectations can lead to disillusionment. For instance, telling everyone that they can achieve the same level of success as a top-tier CEO or a world-renowned athlete, without addressing innate talents, environmental factors, and circumstantial luck, can be a recipe for societal distress. The mental health implications, ranging from feelings of inadequacy to severe depression, can ripple through communities.

Balancing vision with realism is essential, not just for the success of individual endeavors, but also in the larger scheme of societal balance. Life tends to gravitate towards equilibrium states within naturally occurring hierarchical structures. It's an inherent recognition that while leadership roles are crucial, so too are the roles of those who execute the hands-on, day-to-day tasks that keep society functioning. Thus, imagining everyone as a CEO or leader disregards the fundamental principle that an ecosystem thrives on varied contributions. Recognizing these inherent dynamics and limitations isn't a manifestation of pessimism but an approach to informed optimism. It's about pursuing dreams with both fervor and a grounded understanding of the ecosystem's intrinsic needs and structures. After all, even though the success of a football team hinges on the skills of its quarterback and linemen, the foundation of their triumph is built on the indispensable contribution of trainers, coordinators, and even towel managers.

PART FOUR

Dealing with Conflict and Struggle

CHAPTER FOURTEEN

Counter Conflict and the Human Experience

Much like the cunning fox who prefers flight over fight, humans are generally more inclined toward cooperation and peace rather than conflict. We tend to avoid conflict when we can and employ negotiation, compromise, or sometimes retreat as alternative strategies. This characteristic of cooperation has been fundamental to human survival and societal progress, propelling us to become the dominant species on the planet.

This propensity for cooperation is mirrored in studies of human evolutionary biology and psychology. Michael Tomasello's (2014) research on the cooperative nature of human cognition proposes that it is our ability to understand, learn from, and help each other that sets us apart from other species. Furthermore, the prisoner's dilemma, a canonical example in game theory, illustrates how cooperation, despite individual temptations to defect, can lead to optimal outcomes for all involved parties (Axelrod and Hamilton, 1981).

However, analogous to the fox who turns aggressive when cornered, humans may resort to conflict when they feel trapped, threatened, or under extreme stress. Such "cornered" situations can arise in various facets of modern life—at work, in relationships, or in response to societal pressures. Contrary to the fox's physical aggression, though, human aggression often takes the form of emotional or psychological conflict due to social and legal constraints that deter physical violence.

To reconcile these aggressive instincts within societal norms, humans have developed abstract methods of counter conflict. These can include assertive communication, mindfulness practices, or cognitive-behavioral techniques (Beck, 1979). Such practices allow us to process and neutralize threatening stimuli internally before they manifest externally, tempering our more animalistic reactive nature. But this is not necessarily the cut and dry outcome for certain individuals.

Envisioning inner counter-conflict engagement as an inception-like process draws parallels to multiple layers of nested psychological responses. At the outermost layer is the inciting incident or the threat. The initial response might be a primitive, instinctual reaction, the fight-or-flight response etched into our evolutionary biology. It is immediate, reflexive, and not necessarily rational, akin to the fox lashing out when cornered. If the mind is oriented in such a way to resist this impulse intellectually, then the conflict moves inward.

Moving to the next layer, the first counter-conflict arises as we recognize and moderate this impulsive reaction, aided by our prefrontal cortex—the part of the brain associated with higher-order functions like decision-making and impulse

control. We implement strategies of conflict resolution or stress management, trying to neutralize the perceived threat.

However, this may not be the end of the story. Within this second layer exists a third, where the inception deepens. Here, we engage with our feelings about our initial reaction and our subsequent management of it. We might feel guilt about our anger, anxiety about our stress, or conflict about our chosen resolution. This is the realm of meta-emotions—emotions about our emotions (Gottman, Katz, and Hooven, 1996)—which can compound and intensify the original conflict.

This process can spiral further inward, forming even more layers as we react to our meta-emotions, enter meta-cognition—thinking about our thinking (Flavell, 1979)—and potentially get stuck in a cycle of recursive introspection. Herein lies the risk of becoming trapped in these lower tiers of the inception mindset, perpetually reacting to reactions, and feeling emotions about emotions about emotions. It can lead to an infinite regression of self-analysis, which, without productive resolution, could result in chronic stress, anxiety, or other mental health issues.

It's essential to remember that these layers aren't inherently negative. They reflect the depth and complexity of our cognitive and emotional experiences, offering opportunities for introspection, self-awareness, and growth. That being said, it can be a significant challenge to disrupt this recursive cycle of introspection, a process that can lead to considerable discomfort. Drawing a parallel with the concept of the inception, the optimal strategy may be a metaphorical "kick." This "kick" serves to jolt you out of the deep inward spiral, reminiscent of

the mechanism used in Christopher Nolan's film, *Inception*. Just as in the movie, where the "kick" required outside intervention, this process is difficult to do by oneself. Ideally, a trusted friend or family member could be the one to provide this intervention. (Maybe that was the conceptual underpinning of the movie in the first place; never quite thought about it prior to this writing.)

In this context, the "kick" represents a tangible action that pulls you out of the recursive introspection and reconnects you with the physical world. This could be through physical exercise, fulfilling household chores, participating in community service, or addressing other real-world matters. Engaging in these activities can help anchor you in the present moment and shift your focus away from internal contemplation.

A study by Oppezzo and Schwartz (2014) indicates that even simple activities, such as walking, can stimulate creativity and problem-solving abilities. Meanwhile, evidence suggests that volunteering and community service can improve mental health by promoting a sense of purpose and social connection (Piliavin and Siegl, 2007). Even though the abstract issue that initiated the introspection remains, the "kick" helps reset your cognition, no matter how it is initiated. It moves you back from the recursive depths of meta-cognition, allowing you to use cognitive skills—now unencumbered by overthinking— to tackle the issue pragmatically.

For those entangled in the depths of recursive introspection, emerging from it may seem daunting. If simply altering one's thoughts and actions was possible, it would already have been done. Building an adaptive response to this cycle

necessitates an intellectual grasp of the problem and a faith in the existence of a solution. This solution needs to be rooted in clear, accurate information that aligns with the individual's cognitive framework—especially vital for neurodivergent individuals whose cognitive processes might differ from the norm. For instance, individuals with ADHD can significantly benefit from specialized treatment approaches tailored to their distinct neural processing. The most researched and supported treatments for ADHD include parent training in child behavior management and teacher training in classroom management. On the other hand, cognitive-behavioral training for ADHD children has shown limited efficacy, and group social skills training has yielded mixed results. Any therapeutic approach to this and other neurodivergent condition should emphasize the development of treatments grounded in theory, understanding potential side effects of interventions, and unraveling the intricate factors affecting impairments in major life activities to inform subsequent treatment designs. (Antshel and Barkley, 2008).

If creating a personal cognitive "script" that effectively interfaces with your mental heuristics proves challenging, harnessing cognitive biases can be a practical strategy. For instance, the "argument from authority" bias suggests accepting information as true because it comes from a reliable, competent source. Consider this strategy as a form of "borrowed" trust or credibility, which could facilitate belief in a solution and aid in the navigation out of the recursive introspection cycle.

One emotional state in particular can prove to be particularly troubling, so let's explore the construct of shame. Shame is often perceived as an unobtrusive yet powerful tool that subtly influences behavior modification. This uncomfortable sensation of guilt or embarrassment is thought to align an individual's conduct with societal norms and expectations. This perspective is corroborated by evolutionary psychology, suggesting that feelings of shame evolved as a social check to promote group cohesion and survival.

However, the mechanisms of social regulation often stop at inducing feelings of shame, rarely escalating to direct confrontation, especially among those are more passive aggressive. While people may shun or ostracize those who breach societal expectations, overt physical punishment or exclusion are less frequent in modern societies (Fehr and Gachter, 2002). This could be due to the potential disruption to social harmony or because of laws and norms that discourage such actions. Their own intrinsic emotional limitations prove to work towards the benefit of others in this situation.

Given this context, an individual who can recognize and resist these shame-induced emotional responses may have an edge. They could potentially continue to function in environments that might otherwise push them to conformity. This doesn't mean creating overt disruptions or refusing all societal norms, but rather finding a balance—doing just enough to get by without drawing excessive negative attention.

Taking this route might attract some disapproval or scorn from others, but if one can maintain their peace and withstand this pressure, they've essentially found a way to "game" the

social system. A study by T.J. Scheff (2003) suggests that managing and understanding shame can help individuals navigate complex social environments more effectively. Therefore, resilience against shame and the ability to manage societal expectations can be key skills in the modern social landscape, and, for the chronically introspective, offer a modicum of relief from the quagmire of rumination.

While it would undoubtedly be optimal to sidestep circumstances that trigger feelings of shame, practical solutions for such avoidance are often elusive. This is largely because the social ecosystems we inhabit might be fundamentally resistant to our personal influence or escape. For example, family systems or workplace environments may not easily allow for modification or withdrawal, as they're integral parts of our lives.

Confronting shame-inducing situations is a challenging yet ubiquitous aspect of human existence. Drawing from Louis Cozolino's exploration of "The Social Brain," our cognitive and emotional responses are intricately tied to the social fabrics surrounding us (Cozolino, 2014). The profound influence of relationships and early bonding, coupled with underlying neurochemical foundations like oxytocin and dopamine, reveal how deeply our experiences of shame or validation are rooted in both biology and social interaction.

Rather than seeking an escape from these realities, acknowledging and navigating them can lead to resilience and psychological well-being. Cozolino emphasizes that embracing the imperfect intricacies of our social networks, armed with an understanding of their neuro-social constructs,

provides a pragmatic and empowering avenue to handle the complexities of contemporary social life. To actively harness this understanding, it's essential for each of us to foster deeper connections in our communities and prioritize open dialogues about the shared experiences that shape our emotions and thoughts. Engage in introspective practices, such as mindfulness or journaling, to become more attuned to your emotional responses, and seek out supportive groups or therapeutic settings where these insights can be discussed and navigated. By proactively leaning into the social fabric of our existence, not only can we better navigate our own emotions but also become pillars of support for those around us, especially to those who might be having a particularly difficult time overcoming their own shame-based hesitations.

The Dual Edge of Suffering and Existential Awareness: A Comparative Study of Human and Animal Existence

Suffering, deeply woven into our human experience, is as much a part of us as our very consciousness. While we've discussed its link to shame, such emotional responses can arise from various cognitive events. But suffering, when viewed through the lens of purpose, can become a catalyst for growth and resilience. What truly weighs on us is aimless suffering—an endless, seemingly purposeless pain. By channeling this into meaningful action, we can counteract its debilitating effects.

The concept of purpose can be perceived as an orienting property of the brain, much like balance or other senses of perception. Just as our sense of balance ensures our physical equilibrium in our environment, our intrinsic sense of purpose

may guide our cognitive and emotional navigation through our social ecosystem, providing direction and motivation. According to a study by McGregor and Little (1998) in the *Journal of Personality and Social Psychology*, having goals and a clear sense of purpose is linked to a multitude of psychological benefits, suggesting its foundational role in cognitive processing and well-being. Sometimes that sense of purpose can be whatever exists within the absence of extraneous intervening influences.

Consider, for instance, the life of a dairy cow. Even in less-than-ideal conditions, it remains unburdened by existential questions. The cow, unable to conceptualize a different existence, carries on without despair. Its life, though possibly filled with hardships, is relatively straightforward and lacks existential dread, lacking the means to envision a reality beyond its own. It lives its role on a dairy farm and eventually dies, often within 4–6 years.

Humans, on the other hand, are both blessed and burdened with heightened consciousness. We have the gift of longevity, often living over 70 years, yet we grapple continuously with the weight of understanding our existence, and the perceived existence of others around us. Our ability to imagine, to compare, and to dream of other possibilities brings joy, aspiration, and sometimes a great deal of despair, as we are inclined to weigh our current reality against what could be, leading to frustration when our expectations aren't met. Societal narratives further amplify this tension by suggesting that not achieving certain milestones implies a lack of effort or will. This mismatch between our innate capabilities and societal

expectations can sow seeds of self-doubt, especially when we face challenges we aren't inherently equipped to handle.

To some, the dairy cow's life, though physically taxing and short-lived, might seem free from such complexities. It lacks the human burdens of ambition and existential contemplation. While our dreams and aspirations add layers of complexity to our lives, they also infuse it with purpose, meaning, and vibrancy. Our task is to reconcile with this intricate existence, finding meaning amidst the chaos and recognizing our intrinsic boundaries.

Animals inherently follow the path of least resistance, achieving harmony regardless of challenges, since they don't possess a frame of reference for comparison. We will delve into this natural propensity more extensively in the next section. In contrast, humans, shaped by varied life experiences, vacillate between moments of ease and periods of hardship. Such shifts can disrupt our natural equilibrium, a concept we'll examine more closely in the subsequent section.

CHAPTER SIXTEEN

The Principle of Least Resistance: Occam's Razor to Electrical Flow and Beyond

In the realms of both philosophy and physics, a principle has emerged that guides our understanding of systems and their behavior: the principle of least resistance. This principle suggests that when presented with multiple potential paths or solutions, the simplest, most frictionless path tends to be selected. This concept can be found across disciplines, from the theoretical razor of a 14th-century logician to the principles of electrical engineering.

Occam's Razor: The Principle of Parsimony

Occam's Razor is a methodological principle coined by William of Ockham, a logician and Franciscan friar. This principle dictates that, among competing hypotheses that predict equally well, the one with the fewest assumptions should be

selected. Simply put, it emphasizes that simplicity should be prioritized over complexity when all other factors are equal.

Electrical Flow: The Path of Least Resistance

In the field of electrical engineering, the principle of least resistance is quite literal. Electrical current naturally flows along the path of least resistance. This principle forms the foundation of numerous electrical circuits and devices, including resistors, which are electrical components specifically designed to control the path that electricity takes.

Flow States: Least Resistance in Psychology

The principle of least resistance is not confined to the physical or theoretical realms, however. In psychology, the concept of "flow" describes a state of effortless concentration and enjoyment, often referred to as being "in the zone." It's the path of least resistance for the human mind, where the individual is fully absorbed and thoroughly enjoys the process.

When the conditions are right—when challenges are high but matched with appropriate skills—people find themselves immersed in the task at hand, losing sense of time and self-consciousness. Similar to electricity following the path of least resistance, our minds, too, are drawn to the flow state due to its inherently satisfying nature.

However, there is an important distinction that needs to be made here, as sometimes the path of least resistance is illusory. If the perceived state of flow is predicated on falsehoods, assumptions, or some abstract notion that is meant to simulate the experience of stability, then it should be avoided.

It is also worth noting that all real-world circuits have some inherent resistance due to the nature of the materials from which they're made. This resistance arises from the atomic properties of the conductor (whether it's made of copper, silver, etc.) and the interaction of electrons within the material's lattice structure. Even if there are no discrete resistors added to a circuit, the wires and other components themselves will possess some resistance. So, to clarify the metaphor, a certain degree of resistance is inevitable if we seek a directed energy output, that is, to achieve our goals. The Tesla coil serves as a conceptual counterpoint to the metaphor, showcasing a dramatic display of electrical energy, with limited practical use. Prioritize the path where your current flows most effectively and don't let it arc haphazardly into the ether.

Least Resistance: A Universal Principle?

The principle of least resistance has been observed in other scientific disciplines as well, such as in biology, where water and nutrients in plants move along the path of least resistance, or in geology, where rivers carve the path of least resistance through the landscape, driven purely by Earth's gravity.

From these examples, it appears that the principle of least resistance might be a near-universal norm. Whether in the realm of logical reasoning, electrical currents, or human psychology, the propensity towards simplicity, efficiency, and least friction seems to guide the behavior of systems, contributing to their evolution and adaptation.

This principle also provides us with a profound insight into the most efficient and effective ways to solve problems and make decisions. By seeking the simplest, most direct route—by cutting through unnecessary complexities—we can more efficiently reach our goals, mirroring the way electricity finds its path or the way our minds seek the satisfying immersion of the flow state.

Of Mice, Men, and Jars of Flies: Understanding Societal Wellness Through Struggle

John B. Calhoun's famous mouse utopia experiment, conducted in the mid-twentieth century, serves as a remarkable metaphor for societal abundance and its potential pitfalls. Calhoun created a mouse paradise, providing ample food, water, and shelter for his rodent subjects, devoid of threats like predators or disease. But this "utopia" led to surprising results: the mouse population spiraled into destructive behaviors, such as hyper-aggression, cannibalism, and complete social breakdown, ultimately leading to their extinction.

This result contradicts the common assumption that abundance, ease, and security would lead to societal harmony. The experiment suggests that an existence devoid of struggle may, in fact, disrupt social cohesion and individual well-being.

Similarly, the narrative behind the name of Alice in Chains' EP, *Jar of Flies*, offers a poignant, human-centric illustration of a related principle. As band member Jerry Cantrell recounted, one of his childhood teachers conducted an experiment where two jars were filled with flies. One jar was left alone, allowing the flies to fend for themselves, while the other was supplemented with every necessity. Paralleling Calhoun's mouse utopia, the flies in the assisted jar proliferated rapidly but soon perished, while the self-reliant flies in the other jar survived.

Both these anecdotes—one from the realm of science, the other from popular culture—serve as powerful metaphors for the human condition within the context of societal dynamics. They bring into focus the fundamental value of confronting adversity and overcoming hardship. It appears that both mice and men may thrive not in environments of absolute abundance, but in circumstances that require resilience, adaptation, and the courage to confront and overcome challenges.

There exists another illustration worth exploring, rooted in the preservation guidelines of national parks and nature reserves. We are repeatedly reminded not to offer food to the wildlife inhabiting these areas, and the reasoning behind this principle is certainly easy to understand within the contextual dynamics of ease and effort. The animals, given a choice between easy sustenance from human visitors and the energy-intensive task of hunting or foraging, will lean toward the path of least resistance.

This reliance on the easier option, however, comes with serious consequences. The shift away from their natural

instincts toward a reliance on human-provided food alters their behavioral patterns, and this can lead to potential conflicts. As the animals grow bolder in seeking out these easy meals, they might come into escalating, potentially aggressive confrontations with humans. Thus, the seemingly benign act of feeding wild animals can set into motion a chain of events that disturbs the natural order and disrupts the delicate balance of the ecosystem.

In the context of societal wellness, these examples help us acknowledge the importance of struggle and challenge as formative elements in the creation of robust, resilient individuals and societies. While societal support and safety nets are essential for those in positions of abject dispossession, it is equally crucial to avoid creating environments of excessive ease that inadvertently lead to stagnation and decline.

The stories of the mouse utopia, the jar of flies, or the nature of the grizzly bears at your national park could be seen as cautionary indicators for modern societies grappling with issues of abundance and the resulting complacency. They emphasize the necessity for balance—between providing support and encouraging self-reliance, ease and struggle, the comfort of the known and the growth that comes from confronting the unknown. This balance could be the key to a thriving society that promotes not just survival, but the flourishing of its members.

I also think it is worth noting and recognizing an inherent asymmetry in our traditional notions of equilibrium and balance, especially when considering ecosystems or social structures. Life appears more resilient to adversities than to

extended ease. This implies that when presented with two options, we should avoid the simpler route, particularly if it's based on illusions or abstracts, and opt for the more demanding path, especially if it carries fewer assumptions. Imagine a balance beam with its fulcrum shifted to favor one side; when an excess of ease, even just the absence of survival challenges, enters the system, it risks rapid destabilization or collapse. Consider, for instance, how quickly some domesticated species, such as cattle, horses, and pigs, revert to their wild behaviors when reintroduced to their natural habitats. There is an immutable, bold heartiness to life that yearns to be exercised.

The growing popularity of "suffer fests"—such as the Tough Mudder adventure race and the Marathon des Sables ultramarathon—coupled with the immense success of exceptionally challenging video games like *Dark Souls*, indicates that humans often seek out challenges that their daily lives might not offer. The ROM hack community elevates this notion with *Kaizo Mario*, a modified version of Super Mario World, pushing the boundaries of precision platforming and gameplay execution. Completing these challenges offers not only a sense of personal accomplishment but also social capital. This achievement-driven recognition often translates into external validation and potential revenue, aligning closely with the attention economy, a topic we'll delve into later.

CHAPTER EIGHTEEN

The Limits of Liberty

The unstructured, limitless liberty that characterizes many college environments can present a risk to susceptible young minds, making them vulnerable to social contagion, much like a virus in a population with no prior exposure. They often lack the intellectual defenses to resist such pervasive ideological "infections" that can persist for extended periods. Some may eventually develop immunity, but concerning trends suggest that such ideological epidemics may be intensifying with each successive generation.

It's worth noting that Marxism, a philosophy created by Karl Marx—who spent years meandering through academia and hailed from a wealthy family—may reflect the consequence of a privileged viewpoint, crystallized by youthful enthusiasm and naivety. This environment often simplifies complex realities, making simplistic solutions seem attractive. The hubris of youth tends to manifest this outcome in the context of an environment rife with pretense. In the book, *The Coddling of the American Mind: How Good Intentions and Bad Ideas Are Setting Up a Generation for Failure*, scholars Greg Lukianoff and

Jonathan Haidt delve deeply into the repercussions of ideological indoctrination within higher education and its ripple effects throughout society. They underline the dangers of fostering environments where viewpoints go unchallenged, leading to a culture of virtue signaling and echo chambers. These tendencies, they argue, not only stifle intellectual growth and debate but also sow the seeds for societal polarization and misunderstanding. The authors emphasize the importance of open dialogue, critical thinking, and resilience as antidotes to this prevailing trend.

Indeed, it's the allure of simplicity that can often make certain ideologies inherently dangerous. As pattern-seeking animals, we have a natural tendency to gravitate towards solutions that appear clear-cut and straightforward. We often seek shelter in ideas that neatly package the world's complexities into digestible, black-and-white narratives. This inclination is especially strong when faced with uncertainty or adversity, conditions that heighten our need for clarity and coherence.

This is where the cause for concern lies. Complex societal issues, like economic disparities, political polarization, or structural racism, cannot be adequately addressed through oversimplified narratives or "one-size-fits-all" solutions. Such an approach often overlooks the multi-faceted nature of these issues and can lead to ineffective or even harmful policies. Moreover, this kind of thinking can lead to divisions and misunderstandings, as it tends to create false dichotomies and breed intolerance for differing viewpoints. Societies are intricate webs of interconnections and interdependencies, and the problems they face are similarly complex. Effective solutions

require nuanced understanding, open-mindedness, and often, a willingness to navigate the uncomfortable grey areas that simplistic ideologies tend to gloss over.

On a fundamental level of evolutionary biology, it might be taken as a given that absolute freedom is absolutely good. One might think, in seemingly objective fashion, that the absence of restriction is good, so therefore, it is natural and desirable. But why do we have such a proclivity? Is it merely the romanticized idea of liberty that draws us in, or is there something more primal at play? This affinity for absolute freedom, I believe, sprouts from our innate resistance to the shackles that history and society have seemingly placed on us. Over generations, societies have established norms and constraints, and our internalized perceptions of these constraints often feel like chains holding us back from our natural desires and aspirations.

Think of it as a pendulum. On one side, we have our history, rich with tales of oppression, subjugation, and societal constructs that have tried to curtail or modify human behavior. In response, the pendulum swings to the other extreme, giving rise to a fervent yearning for limitless freedom, because one might find himself thinking, "I absolutely hate this current experience, so the preferred alternative would be the polar opposite." This resistance, this impulse to break free, is primal. It's akin to a wild animal caged and yearning to roam free in its natural habitat.

But life, with its inherent hardships, is already a formidable challenge. When added layers of perceived societal injustices or constraints come into play, our natural reaction is to resist,

to push back against what feels like an added burden. But interestingly, there are those among us who view societal structures in a different light: as mere extensions or analogues to nature's own checks and balances. To them, societal norms are no different than the rules nature lays down: the need to hunt for food or the instinct to avoid predation.

It's a perspective worth pondering. Just as animals don't philosophically resist the need to hunt or hide—they simply act on these instincts—perhaps we, too, should consider whether some of our societal constructs are simply pragmatic responses to the broader challenges of coexistence and survival. Rather than seeing them as oppressive shackles, could we view them as necessary guidelines, much like the rules of nature, designed to help us navigate our collective journey more harmoniously?

PART FIVE

Society, Culture, and the Individual

CHAPTER NINETEEN

An Individual Journey of Societal Rejection

Christopher McCandless's tale, told compellingly in Jon Krakauer's *Into the Wild*, demonstrates the dire consequences of rebelling against societal norms. A parallel can be drawn to the narratives of Beatnik authors, the infamous Unabomber Ted Kaczynski, and Salinger's Holden Caulfield. These figures, like McCandless, defied societal conventions, though McCandless's defiance resulted in his own tragic end.

McCandless's story is not just an individual tragedy but a reflection of a larger societal trend, the intense resistance to the ongoing evolution of human society. He stands as a symbol for those feeling estranged by societal structures and choosing their unique paths. His decision to completely sever ties with society and embrace the wilderness underscores his preference for the raw simplicity of survival over the perceived complexities of modern existence. The Unabomber, sharing this sentiment of extreme detachment, may have been

closer ideological kin to McCandless than other counterculture figures who chose to remain within societal confines, albeit grudgingly. McCandless's fate, however, uniquely exemplifies the potential peril of total societal disconnection. While the Unabomber's actions—being something of a terrorist campaign against that which he perceived to be the root cause of societal ills—ultimately led to life imprisonment and eventual death, McCandless's personal journey ended in a wilderness ordeal that some might interpret as a self-inflicted demise.

Through figures like McCandless and Kaczynski, we see another interplay between personal authenticity and societal connection. While embracing individuality is crucial, extreme isolation or rebellion can lead to dire outcomes. It's essential to recognize our roles within a larger community and the wisdom it provides. By understanding this balance, we can lead enriched lives that serve both our personal aspirations and the greater good.

Disenchantment, Countercultures, and the Search for a Sustainable Structure

A sense of disillusionment often arises when individuals feel powerless to affect change, are marginalized by the lack of opportunity, or find themselves estranged from their community or broader society. This despondency is vividly reflected in the writings of Beatnik authors from the 1950s, as well as in J.D. Salinger's character, Holden Caulfield, from *The Catcher in the Rye*. The striking commonality among these instances is not about struggling against imminent threats to survival or battling specific oppression. Instead, it's the philosophical alienation from the societal state that fuels their despair.

While the specific rationalizations for their views varied, a general resistance to the established structure and spirit of the 20th-century post-war American culture was prevalent. This could be viewed as an emergent sociological evolutionary

reaction to a perceived unfair game at a deep, subconscious level. To counteract this perceived unfairness, these individuals either created a counterculture or aligned with existing ones. Even in these instances, a structure emerges; however, it is one that they perceive as being based on fairer terms. Yet, the creation of such countercultures often leads to an unsustainable situation. It allows for a proliferation of ideological factions that splinter off to establish their own versions of society, leading to fragmentation and instability. In this scenario, the pursuit of freedom becomes disabling. When circumstances do not align with a person's self-centric view, it can lead to a continual regression, as they seek out or attempt to create new environments that do.

The answer to such disillusionment and despondency may not necessarily lie in resisting or withdrawing from societal structures but in finding a personal purpose within them. By identifying a cornerstone of purpose within the existing sociological framework, individuals can develop a more reliable and sustainable structure for long-term fulfillment. This approach not only provides a path towards personal growth but also contributes to the growth of society as a macro-organism.

When individuals find their purpose within the broader societal structure, they are not simply working towards their own self-fulfillment. They are contributing to a larger, shared vision that extends beyond their personal scope. By doing so, they strengthen the societal fabric, enriching it with diverse experiences and perspectives. Therefore, disillusionment can be mitigated not by eschewing societal structures, but by actively engaging with them, carving a personal niche that aligns

with larger social goals. In this way, the pursuit of personal fulfillment and societal development becomes a mutual, symbiotic process, leading towards a healthier, more holistic growth for all.

Nevertheless, Holden Caulfield, or at least the essence and ideology that the literary character embodies, represents an industrial society archetype that manifests and reiterates over the expanse of experience that has transpired since his inception. For example, Ted Kaczynski, known as the Unabomber, seemingly embodies the same form of alienation and dissatisfaction with society. Holden's character, while fictional, has long been emblematic of the disenchanted youth. His disillusionment, anxiety, and his sense of being an outsider echo the existential angst that has been associated with Kaczynski.

Holden's world view is entrenched in a binary perception of "phony" vs. "authentic," with the majority of the world falling into the former category. This binary mirrors Kaczynski's dichotomous perception of society as divided into technophiles (those who embrace modern technology) and those like himself, who reject it vehemently. Both of them idealize a more "authentic" existence away from what they perceive as the falseness of modern society. From a sociological standpoint, both Kaczynski and Caulfield exhibit strong anti-establishment sentiments, a clear critique of the societal structures they found themselves in. Kaczynski's manifesto, *Industrial Society and Its Future*, rails against the modern technological society, not unlike Caulfield's disdain for the "phoniness" of postwar America. However, their responses to these perceived ills varied greatly.

Holden's rebellion is passive-aggressive and primarily internal. His resistance to growing up and his attempt to protect children from the adult world represent a rejection of societal norms and expectations. He embodies what sociologists refer to as "role strain"—the tension one experiences when they struggle to meet the numerous demands of a particular role—in his case, adulthood.

Kaczynski, on the other hand, externalized his discontent in a manner far more destructive and criminal, resorting to bombing as a means of conveying his ideological point of view against industrial-technological society. His acts were driven by a radical form of social alienation and were a manifestation of his profound disconnection from society, demonstrating the extreme lengths some individuals may go when they feel utterly estranged. He made cogent points about the nature of industrialized society, though he was woefully ineffective at actualizing his goals. He exists as a testament to the notions previously discussed regarding knowing what game you're playing or what ecosystem you occupy, and having the presence of mind to either find a new approach or shift your paradigm so you don't feel compelled to mail pipe bombs to your ideological opponents.

CHAPTER TWENTY-ONE

Understanding the Complex Dynamics of Modern Dating and Beyond

The essence of human connection, it could be argued, is simpler than we often conceive it to be. We, as humans, seem innately driven to infuse complexity into the equation, possibly due to ego-driven perspectives or the discomfort stemming from cognitive dissonance.

Consider, for instance, when we find a match on a digital dating platform. The mental gymnastics commence as we begin to speculate about the other party's perception of us. Should we harbor specific intentions—be they romantic, sexual, or otherwise—we may feel inclined to amplify those characteristics we believe would resonate with the other person, based on our interpretations of their profile. An individual blessed with the skill of acting and a dose of intellectual empathy may convincingly perform such a charade for a significant period. However, if the behaviors enacted do not spring

from an authentic place within their persona, the weight of maintaining this façade may eventually prove emotionally overwhelming. Sustaining a performance that strays too far from our core self can be a draining task indeed, casting light on the simplicity and ease of genuine interaction.

When we encounter a relational dynamic where our traits seem to fall short of our partner's desires or expectations, we might feel compelled to manufacture a change within ourselves. This could be motivated by the dread of solitude or a desire to avoid the perceived failure of relationship dissolution. Yet, it is critical to remember that we are not universally compatible, just as not all are suitable matches for us. Natural selection, the unseen force guiding the course of life, weaves a multitude of intricate paths. Some endure for epochs; others extinguish within mere generations. It operates without any subjective inclination, shaping reality in a way that simply "is." Should a prospective partner reject you forthwith, resist the urge to dissect the reasons they provide.

Despite these theoretical deliberations, the brutal truth remains: the inexorable engine of natural selection may not have earmarked a union between you and a specific individual. This becomes particularly evident when we scrutinize the world of online dating. In this vast ocean of prospective matches, we see the "law of averages" unfolding right before our eyes. This terminology alludes not only to the statistical principle but also suggests that a significant majority of app users fall within the bell curve of societal beauty standards. Consequently, these platforms inadvertently reveal the stochastic essence of our romantic pursuits.

Venturing forth into this sea teeming with potential companions, one inevitably encounters challenges akin to the "red flags" in a slalom skiing contest. Just as these flags add an element of complexity to the race, hurdles encountered during the dating journey can make the pursuit more intriguing. Successfully navigating these obstacles in both scenarios can impart a thrilling sense of accomplishment. However, it is crucial to distinguish between the stakes involved in these two distinct experiences.

In slalom skiing, a red flag indicates a sharp turn that requires skillful maneuvering. Accepting and conquering these challenges are part of the sport, and skiers who complete the course despite the obstacles are often applauded for their skill and courage. Similarly, overcoming challenges in relationships can lead to a sense of personal growth and accomplishment.

Even though it may unironically be considered a sport-like activity to many, the "red flags" in dating usually signal potential harm or incompatibility, which, if ignored, might lead to emotional distress or, in worst-case scenarios, abusive relationships. It is, therefore, crucial to recognize that not all "flags" are meant to be challenged or conquered. Because in both cases, even if you consider yourself an expert of the "slopes," hubris can be our ultimate undoing. As the Proverb says, "Pride goeth before destruction, and a haughty spirit before a fall."

While resilience, adaptability, and the capacity to compromise are valuable traits to possess in any context, it's important to draw the line at tolerating behaviors or traits that are detrimental to one's emotional well-being or fundamental

values. Dating should not be about surviving a gauntlet of red flags, but rather about seeking a partner with whom one can build a healthy and mutually fulfilling relationship. Now if that sounds boring to you, then you're probably going to die on those slopes, one way or another.

So, while we can draw mild amusement from the metaphor of the slalom skier's courage and determination, we should also be mindful of our well-being. Recognize and respect the red flags in your dating journey and remember: the goal isn't just to reach the bottom of the most challenging slope in record time, but to enjoy the ride along the way. Though if you do consider yourself an Olympic gold medalist at this particular activity, consider quitting while you still have all of your appendages and possessions intact, especially as the man-made climate change fundamentally alters the landscape of the slope itself.

Physical attractiveness does hold a potent sway in our social dynamics, often influencing the attention one receives, and partially or significantly downplaying the acknowledgment of a red flag. Men and women alike may indeed overlook or tolerate certain behaviors if they find the other person sufficiently appealing. Additionally, social media and the rise of online platforms have amplified this phenomenon by prioritizing aesthetics and facilitating a culture of constant comparison.

For men who may not meet traditional standards of attractiveness, society often expects them to offer other value-adding elements, such as financial stability or a riveting personality that can yield socially shareable experiences. But even

these traits may not guarantee lasting interest, due to the high competition dating landscape shaped by the abundance of choices available through social media and dating apps. Women, especially those deemed conventionally attractive, are granted the luxury of having a variety of options with very little expectation placed upon them, because their market valuation is quite high (Medium.com, 2015). This, coupled with an increasingly individualistic society that encourages the pursuit of personal fulfillment, results in a dwindling inclination to invest time and effort in maintaining long-term relationships. For some, the lure of experiencing short-lived, ego-boosting relationships becomes more appealing.

This narrative might sound cynical and arguably oversimplified. Still, it's a reflection of how societal norms, media influence, and our innate biological tendencies can interact and shape our behavior in the realm of dating and relationships. Detractors of this notion would say it's important to note that while these trends might be observable in some societal segments, they do not represent the entirety of human relationships and interactions, and that many individuals still value authenticity, emotional connection, and shared values when choosing a partner. But it would be difficult to prove that those notions are even concrete elements of reality, and not just the simulated products of conditioned internal narrative development. It would be so easy for a person to say they desire authenticity if the surrounding community also claims to value that particular trait, without fundamentally understanding what it is they're asserting.

The world of online dating embodies the quintessence of postmodern relativity. It's a realm where a multiplicity of perspectives, desires, and identities coalesces, resulting in an astonishing range of potential matches and mismatches. The detailed bio enthusiast may find intellectual stimulation in the open book approach, appreciating the immediate insight into a prospective partner's personality, passions, and peculiarities. Meanwhile, fans of the minimalistic profile may relish the mystery, the slow uncovering of layers over time, believing that people cannot be adequately encapsulated in a limited bio.

Diversity is further pronounced when we examine attributes like physical appearance, personal beliefs, and idiosyncrasies. Some are attracted to traditional beauty norms, while others may seek unconventional allure, challenging the societal status quo. Likewise, dating participants may gravitate towards potential partners who share similar worldviews, religions, or political inclinations. Conversely, they may yearn for a connection with those who bring a different perspective, hoping for a broadening and enriching of their own understanding.

Ultimately, the beauty of online dating lies in its ability to cater to all these divergent preferences. Just like the wider debates in society, the online dating arena validates the idea that there's no one-size-fits-all answer, but rather multiple solutions shaped by individual perceptions and experiences.

Our preferences and inclinations, much like physical existence, are not stagnant but constantly evolving entities. They shift and mutate under the influence of personal experiences, evolving societal norms, cultural trends, and the ever-changing landscape of our individual growth.

These transformations, in turn, pervade every facet of our existence, from the nuances of our interpersonal relationships to the way we consume and perceive the world around us. They shape our communication styles, our interactions, our consumer patterns, and, indeed, our romantic choices.

However, this fluidity of preference presents an intriguing conundrum: in a world where tastes and trends can pivot at a moment's notice, prediction and customization become a game of strategic guesswork. Yes, one may be able to capture the zeitgeist and ride the wave of short-term success. Yet, this victory is often fleeting, elusive—as elusive as the ever-changing tides of public sentiment and personal growth.

In this light, a product, an idea, or an individual can either align with the currents of the market or societal milieu, or they might find themselves at odds with it. Adapting to the changing whims might provide intermittent victories, but it's worth noting that the very fabric of life thrives on unpredictability, capable of overthrowing even the most meticulously crafted plans and strategies.

This reality invites us to consider a profound truth—rather than perpetually striving to adapt or conform, perhaps there's inherent value in authenticity, in resonating with an audience or market not because we've morphed ourselves to fit into their box, but because who we are intrinsically aligns with what they seek.

While humans may believe they have mastered understanding and prediction, such notions might be more reflective of our need for control than an actual grasp of reality. As mentioned, many times in many ways throughout this book,

we are products of our genetic make-up and environment, shaped by myriad influences that give us the impression of understanding. Yet, this understanding could be merely surface-level, akin to the prisoners in Plato's allegory of the cave who mistake shadows for reality. In a world devoid of alternate timelines to compare outcomes, absolute certainty remains elusive. However, when you deconstruct life to its core elements—matter, energy, and the processes they undergo—it becomes apparent that causality is the driving force behind our macroscopic experience of reality. Our experiences are simply emergent properties of these fundamental processes. While it's a humbling perspective, it's also a compelling reminder of our interconnectedness with the universe and its ceaseless dance of cause and effect.

CHAPTER TWENTY-TWO

Cultural Consequences of Isolation

In the late 20th and early 21st centuries, a distinct set of auditory trends began to emerge, seeming to simultaneously reflect and shape the cultural zeitgeist. Notably, phenomena such as the ASMR movement, the rise of breathy vocals in popular music, and the proliferation of headphone usage began to intertwine with reported feelings of isolation, especially among the Millennial and Gen Z generations.

Autonomous Sensory Meridian Response (ASMR), characterized by soft-spoken words, whispers, and tactile sound effects, has captivated vast online audiences. Described as inducing a tingling sensation in its listeners, ASMR videos seem to cater to a deep-seated need for sensory intimacy and comfort. Amidst the cacophony of the digital age, where sensory overload is commonplace, ASMR stands out as a curated oasis of calm. These auditory experiences, delivered in whispers and soft tones, provide a sharp contrast to the ambient noise of daily life and offer a form of sensory refuge.

Parallel to the ASMR movement is the increasing preference in popular music for breathy, almost whispered vocals. Unlike the clear, powerful vocal delivery of earlier decades, this style conveys vulnerability and raw emotion. It speaks to a generation that values authenticity, resonating with those who feel disconnected from the highly produced and curated images of perfection that flood their digital lives. This is not just about music but an auditory reflection of the yearning for genuine human connection and emotional rawness.

Integral to both these phenomena is the medium through which they are most often consumed: headphones. With advances in technology, especially noise-cancelling capabilities, headphones allow for the creation of personal sound sanctuaries. They offer both a retreat from external distractions and an immersive experience into chosen auditory worlds. More than just tools for sound consumption, headphones have become social signals, subtly indicating a person's current availability or desire for solitude. In a world teeming with stimuli, headphones grant agency to the listener, allowing them to control their auditory environment.

Yet, it is essential to consider these trends in light of broader societal shifts. Increasingly, reports highlight the loneliness and feelings of isolation experienced by Millennials and Gen Z. These are generations that came of age in the digital era, with unparalleled technological connectivity. Paradoxically, while the world is more connected than ever, genuine interpersonal connections seem to be dwindling. Physical interactions and traditional communal bonds have seen a

decline, often replaced by virtual interactions and digital communities.

The overlap of these auditory preferences and generational feelings of solitude isn't mere coincidence. The intimate nature of ASMR, the emotional authenticity conveyed by breathy vocals, and the personal soundscapes created by headphones, all seem to cater to a deep-seated need for connection and intimacy in an era characterized by emotional distance. They act as auditory anchors, providing comfort and solace amidst the tumult of modern life.

In essence, the complex interplay of these auditory trends and societal shifts underscores the evolving ways in which culture and individual needs influence and reflect each other. They serve as reminders of the enduring human need for connection, intimacy, and sensory comfort, even as the avenues for fulfilling these needs continue to evolve.

However, I've always felt a degree of visceral unease with ASMR, not just because of the sounds or the format, but with the way it has captivated people's attention in such an unnatural manner. Followers of these content creators will often comment how the content gives them something to look forward to, or helps them through moments of grief or loss. These people are so bereft of support in their analogue lives that they invest their reality into strangers speaking softly and giving them the illusion of attention. I think this sets the precedent for what we should expect to see in the near future, which is the progressive development of siloed modes of living, interacting with virtual avatars and analogues at increasing frequency. After all, this is the path of least resistance:

requiring the least amount of effort and bears the most mini-
mal amount of vulnerable discomfort. As we discussed previously, the path of least resistance shows up in various instances within nature, so reframing our perspective on human
behavior with this lens may help us decipher our nature with
greater clarity. After exploring the intricacies of auditory
trends and how they mirror the emotional nuances of contemporary society, it's essential to turn our attention to another
dimension of cultural discourse that continues to shape collective perceptions and attitudes: the realm of societal privilege and its multifaceted implications.

CHAPTER TWENTY-THREE

The Ideological Vulnerability of Privilege: An Examination of "White Guilt"

The concept of privilege, particularly as it pertains to social hierarchies, is well-established yet profoundly complex. For instance, white liberals, who have traditionally occupied a dominant position in society, often encounter unique dilemmas. Having benefitted from generations of privilege and relatively unchallenged majority demographics, their ideological resilience may be tested, similar to how an organism might be vulnerable to foreign pathogens that threaten its biological stability.

This vulnerability could contribute to phenomena such as "white guilt," a sense of personal culpability for historical injustices committed by one's ancestors. This is a peculiar sociological phenomenon, as it does not neatly correspond to concepts of personal responsibility or contemporary societal norms. Throughout history, most substantial ethnic or

national groups have committed some form of atrocity. As such, persistently adopting a mentality of historical victimhood might be counterproductive.

Addressing injustice is undoubtedly vital. Yet, it's equally important to steer clear of simplistic solution-oriented thinking that often resorts to sweeping generalizations about certain demographics. It's crucial to bear in mind that it was specific individuals, not entire demographic groups, who were accountable for historical atrocities. Attributing guilt to the distant descendants for the actions of their ancestors may fuel further division instead of promoting understanding and unity.

The religious doctrine of Original Sin in Catholic theology resonates with the idea of inherited guilt. Parallels exist between this doctrine and modern ideologies advocating for collective guilt over past injustices, potentially promoting division and resentment (Branscombe, Schmitt, & Schiffhauer, 2007). The Branscombe study found that white Americans who strongly identify with their racial category tend to express heightened modern racism when reflecting on their racial privilege. Conversely, those with low racial identification tend to exhibit less racism, highlighting the dangers of assigning blame based on broad identity markers. In short, overemphasizing a uniform perception of racial identity can be counterproductive, as it may exacerbate the issue being addressed, or create new dimensions of societal strife. Civilization would benefit more from promoting understanding and unity rather than emphasizing inherited guilt.

While recognizing the historic record remains a cornerstone of honest dialogue, we must actively avoid placing the weight of our ancestors' actions on today's individuals. Let's prioritize personal accountability and address today's challenges with practical, open-minded discourse, paving the way for a society built on understanding and collaboration rather than guilt and blame.

CHAPTER TWENTY-FOUR

The Complexity of Transgenderism and the Interplay of Societal Forces

The topic of transgenderism is complex and multifaceted, involving the interaction of biology, identity, societal norms, and power structures. Public discourse in recent years seems to over-emphasize the narratives of individuals transitioning from male to female (MTF), somewhat overshadowing those transitioning from female to male (FTM). This discrepancy might be reflecting various cultural dynamics at work (Schilt & Westbrook, 2009).

One theory proposes that some transgender women (MTF) might maintain, consciously or subconsciously, traditional masculine behaviors, such as assertiveness and dominance. These behaviors could be residues of their initial socialization or could stem from innate biological factors (Beemyn & Rankin, 2011). If these individuals are indeed deploying these traits to advocate for their rights and representation,

it could partly account for the overrepresentation of transgender women in media and popular culture.

The present social climate, shaped in part by 4th wave feminism, encourages the deconstruction of traditional gender roles and characteristics, while still accentuating the preeminence of the concept of the "woman" (Cooper, 2016). While this has fostered greater gender fluidity and promotes personal acceptance, it has also redefined societal expectations for masculinity, associating it with traits such as emotional openness, empathy, and flexibility.

Under these influences, some biological males might feel the urge to align with the emerging societal norms, integrating these newly celebrated traits into their identities. This evolution serves to maintain their social standing in a rapidly evolving society (Nagoshi & Brzuzy, 2010). For those identifying as transgender, transitioning might be a critical part of this adaptation, aligning their internal identity with society's shifting expectations. It is compelling to consider society's tendency to prioritize the abstract concept of "womanhood" over practical considerations or logical reasoning, especially when disregarding the inherent physical advantages of biological males in contexts like women's sports competitions. But this creates a clear opportunity for exploitation from those who seek to utilize the skewed playing field to their advantage. Referencing the earlier visualization of the "whys" and "why nots," I think we are seeing an instance where the "why nots" are proliferating, as the abstract notion of social acceptance and equity are winning out over objective "why" rebuttals, due to the social capital valuation of virtue signaling. Though in that sense,

the ends justify the means, creating an ulterior "why" motivation for those progressive advocates.

One interesting point of comparison exists within another member of the animal kingdom, namely the giant cuttlefish. It is a remarkable cephalopod known not just for its mesmerizing display of colors and patterns, but also for its intriguing mating strategies. Among these fascinating creatures, smaller males have developed a clever tactic to increase their mating chances. To evade competition with larger, more dominant males, these smaller males mimic the appearance and behavior of females, allowing them the chance to discreetly approach and mate with females right under the noses of their unsuspecting rivals. This ingenious tactic showcases the adaptive creativity of the animal kingdom in the ever-challenging game of reproduction. Could the trends we notice in contemporary society be in some way linked to evolutionary strategies like these mating behaviors?

We stand at a pivotal juncture, akin to the very fringes of the universe, as we grapple with the intricacies of gender, race, and the overarching theme of intersectionality. Just as our ancient predecessors dared to venture into the vastness of the ocean, long before they grasped the intricacies of navigation or the looming threats of the deep, we, too, embark on a journey to understand complex societal constructs. When pondering the potential void or infinite expanse at the universe's edge, one can't help but wonder what lies beyond our current understanding. Will our exploration reveal more layers of complexity and meaning, or will it confirm that our current

boundaries of knowledge are truly the final frontier, with nothing more profound lying beyond?

CHAPTER TWENTY-FIVE

The Cultural Complexity of Transgender Identity: A Comparative View

In the modern landscape of identity politics, transgender-ism presents a particularly complex dynamic. Viewed through one lens, it can be perceived as adding a layer of complexity to our social interactions, transforming a traditionally binary system into a highly individualized and fluid construct, dependent on each person's unique interpretation and self-identification. Much like a bureaucracy with its extensive rules and regulations, the evolving notion of gender identity introduces numerous subjective nuances, not easily classified into pre-existing societal norms or intuitively understood. This fluidity, while promoting a greater professed sense of personal authenticity, also necessitates a more intricate system of interpersonal recognition.

Imagine, for instance, a hypothetical scenario in which individuals would need to share a detailed "identity

questionnaire" upon meeting, specifying their gender identity, pronouns, and other demographic details, to ensure appropriate and respectful interaction. This level of specificity may seem cumbersome or overly formalized to some, mirroring the tensions present in any bureaucratic system, but it's not a stretch to believe that some might earnestly advocate for this model to be implemented into daily discourse and social engagement.

Furthermore, this system of individualized identity, much like any other form of social bureaucracy, is not immune to potential power dynamics. Some individuals might wield their identity class as a tool to exert authority or control over others, under the pretense of advocating for inclusivity and respect. This parallels how government systems, while designed to serve public interests, can often become entangled in power struggles and inefficiencies.

CHAPTER TWENTY-SIX

Gender, Emotional Intelligence, and Societal Perceptions

We stand at the threshold of a significant sociocultural transformation, profoundly influenced by the expanding research and personal accounts related to mental health. More individuals than ever are seeking to understand their personal realities, striving for a distinct identity within the vast landscape of human experience. This journey extends beyond just interpreting societal gender norms; it's a deeper quest to understand the factors that establish and perpetuate them. Within sociology, there are notable comparisons and differences between the increased prevalence of autism in men and traditional gender expectations.

A common perception is that men, on average, exhibit lower emotional intelligence than women. While this broad generalization isn't universally accurate, numerous neuroscientific studies have found unique neurological and hormonal elements that might impact the development of empathy in

men, especially those diagnosed with conditions like Autism Spectrum Disorder (ASD) (Baron-Cohen, 2002).

Examining the prevalence of autism among men, a wealth of research indicates a higher incidence of ASD in males, often reflected in a male-to-female ratio of about 3:1 (Loomes, 2017). The root causes behind this gender disparity are yet to be definitively identified, but proposed explanations often encompass genetic, hormonal, and environmental factors (Werling & Geschwind, 2013). The 'extreme male brain' theory suggests that females with Autism Spectrum Conditions may display behaviors commonly associated with male neurology. In a study aimed at understanding this, AQ scores from various groups—including transmen, transwomen, typical males, typical females, and individuals with Asperger Syndrome—were compared. Findings indicated that transmen scored higher on the AQ than typical females, males, and transwomen but lower than those with Asperger Syndrome. This data implies that transmen might exhibit more autistic traits, possibly impacting how they socially engage with female peers and leading to a closer identification with male social groups.

It's intriguing to consider that autism may reinforce traditional masculine norms for men while simultaneously influencing women to lean into their perception of culturally-defined masculinity, even amidst concerns of its toxic elements. However, a significant factor to consider is biological women who identify as transgender yet also embrace a non-binary identity. This may suggest that societal pressures drive some individuals to adopt more fluid and undefined labels. This phenomenon somewhat reminds me of the 90s' cultural shift

against rigid classifications. Even though these individuals are drawn to labels, they prefer to define them on their own terms rather than letting society dictate their meaning.

Conversely, traditional gender roles have changed across different times and cultures, often setting particular behavioral standards for men, such as emotional restraint, independence, assertiveness, and analytical thinking. Historically, many societies have socialized men to control their emotions, assume leadership roles, and cultivate a competitive demeanor.

However, some individuals with autism might find it challenging to align with these conventional gender expectations. For example, the general practice of emotional restraint might not resonate with many autistic individuals who, despite facing difficulties in understanding and communicating emotions, often feel them deeply. The societal expectation for dominance could conflict with the social challenges they experience. Yet, the analytical and detail-oriented thinking, commonly associated with ASD, might resonate well with the problem-solving attributes traditionally expected of men. The difference in ASD prevalence and its interaction with societal expectations for men introduces a host of sociological questions. For instance, how does society accommodate or stigmatize the traits associated with autism? How do these gender norms affect the diagnosis rates? And more importantly, how does it shape the lived experiences of men with autism? In unraveling these questions, we begin to appreciate the need for more nuanced understandings of societal expectations and neurodiversity.

Research posits that men might exhibit a distinct blend of cognitive and emotional traits that can include a lower aggregate emotional intelligence, heightened aggression, and a statistically higher propensity towards certain cognitive shortcomings related to IQ (Baron-Cohen, 2002; Archer, 2004; Deary et al., 2007). Hormonal chemistry, specifically the influence of testosterone, may augment these characteristics (Denson, Mehta, & Ho Tan, 2013). Thus, the errors or misguided decisions undertaken by men might sometimes manifest as more conspicuous outcomes, fostering the perception that men are more susceptible to mistakes or irrational actions. Nevertheless, it's critical to remember that this doesn't represent all men. Often, the actions of a few create enduring impressions, leading to harmful stereotypes (Fiske, Cuddy, Glick, & Xu, 2002). Amplifying the negative actions of a subset of individuals within a group can lead to unfairly skewed perceptions of that entire group.

Such stereotypes might be one of the reasons men, particularly those in positions of privilege, become targets for criticism, notably among liberal circles. This could explain why any suggestion of privilege within this demographic often seems to draw criticism and contempt. Just as it is inappropriate to hold modern individuals accountable for historical injustices committed by their ancestors, it is also unhelpful to attribute negative characteristics universally to men based on the actions of a subset of individuals.

As a society, we need to strive for a deeper sense of understanding, looking beyond stereotypes and generalizations. Recognizing individual accountability, promoting empathy,

and understanding the complex interplay of biology, psychology, and society can help foster a more balanced and less divisive view of all individuals, regardless of their gender.

From social conditioning, certain individuals seem to operate under the assumption that being aggressive or confrontational establishes their authority and compels others to respect their demands. While such a forceful approach can occasionally secure short-term advantages, it generally sows seeds of resentment and negativity, affecting one's quality of life in the long term by embittering perceptions about specific personality types and social or professional situations.

On the other hand, individuals who are overly agreeable may risk being exploited. However, by maintaining a positive, cooperative attitude, they contribute to a more pleasant overall environment, which can have long-term benefits. The key, then, lies in striking a balance: appreciate and show gratitude for opportunities (in work, relationships, and so on) but assert your needs and boundaries in a manner that preserves harmony. From a sociological perspective, this is the most beneficial approach for society at large.

The counterargument revolves around the mindset of scarcity or desperation, where individuals feel compelled to seize every opportunity, fearing it may not come again. This mindset can foster aggressive, "beta male" behavior, as individuals feel forced to resort to oppressive power dynamics to assert themselves. This can be a survival strategy, predicated on the notion that these types might not survive in the wild, so they resort to these tactics.

To reiterate, a society that has not recently experienced oppressive behavior or tyranny may be ill-equipped to recognize and respond to behaviors that genuinely threaten to undermine the stability of society. This underscores the need for awareness and understanding of these dynamics to ensure healthy and productive social interactions. Though perhaps this creates something of a perpetually circulating vision of reality: crises in society create the need for forceful action, the persistence of the action is eventually seen as unnecessary once the perceived threats subside, so the ensuing peacetime essentially precipitates the conditions for the crisis to emerge again.

CHAPTER TWENTY-SEVEN

Postmodernism and the Transgender Movement: A Confluence of Concepts

Postmodernism, a philosophical movement that originated in the mid-20th century, champions the idea of deconstructing established narratives and binaries. It emphasizes subjectivity, relativity, and the fragmentation of cultural constructs. In many ways, the contemporary transgender movement can be seen as an embodiment of these postmodernist principles, as it actively challenges and redefines traditional norms surrounding gender identity.

In the postmodernist lens, gender isn't viewed as a strict binary—male or female—but rather as a spectrum of identities that can be fluid and changing. This outlook aligns closely with the perspectives of many within the transgender community, who advocate for a broader understanding of gender that encompasses diverse identities beyond just "male" and "female." The emphasis on individual subjectivity and personal

self-definition is a core element of both postmodernist thought and the transgender movement.

Another postmodernist idea reflected in the transgender movement is the critique of universal meta-narratives, or overarching stories that seek to explain societal or cultural phenomena. Postmodernists argue that these narratives often exclude or marginalize certain voices and perspectives. Similarly, the transgender movement challenges the dominant narrative of a binary gender system, arguing that this view erases or marginalizes those who don't fit neatly into the categories of "male" or "female."

In addition, both postmodernism and the transgender movement stress the importance of language in shaping our understanding of the world. For postmodernists, language is seen as a powerful tool for constructing reality, rather than merely describing it. This notion is mirrored in the discourse of the transgender movement, which emphasizes the power of language and self-identification in shaping an individual's gender identity.

In essence, the principles of postmodernism—deconstruction of binaries, critique of meta-narratives, subjectivity, and the power of language—are visibly manifest in the practices and philosophies of the transgender movement. In challenging established norms and advocating for a more inclusive understanding of gender, the transgender movement can be viewed as a living embodiment of postmodernist philosophy.

CHAPTER TWENTY-EIGHT

The Dynamics of Conservative and Liberal Perspectives: Status Quo, Change, and Emotional States

Conservatives and liberals have been known to approach change differently: conservatives often react to changes beyond their control, striving to preserve the status quo and maintain equilibrium, whereas liberals tend to be proactive agents of change, spurred by dissatisfaction with aspects of the present they believe should be different.

However, when actions stem from emotionally charged states, they risk being less objective and potentially harmful, particularly if underpinned by misinformation or deceit. These reactive or proactive changes can inadvertently merely replace an existing hierarchical structure with a new one, shrouded in a different power dynamic. This perpetuation of power dynamics, merely under a new guise, doesn't resolve the

perceived inequities; rather, it rearranges the players in the power game.

Those who find themselves disadvantaged by the current hierarchy often perceive it as an unfair power structure to be dismantled, with the hope that they might benefit from the ensuing power vacuum. The hope lies in the potential to gain an upper hand in whatever the new structure happens to be. This perspective falls into a pitfall: the pursuit of change for the sake of change, instead of progress. True societal improvement necessitates changes that are objectively positive, fair, and considerate of the complexities of societal structures. Otherwise, we merely shuffle the same deck of cards, without altering the game's inherent inequities. There's an inherent balance between preserving the established order and adapting to new circumstances. Just as a river's course is ever-changing yet defined by its banks, so too is the fluidity of societal perspectives. The role of a rational mind is to navigate these waters with purpose and discernment. Merely shifting power dynamics without understanding the essence of power is akin to being adrift without direction. True societal progression isn't just in rearranging authority but in a profound comprehension of the nature of power and influence. A society should strive not merely to change its leadership but to ensure that governance embodies justice, wisdom, and the collective good. The true essence of progress lies not in who holds power, but in how it's wielded to uplift and align with enduring virtues.

PART SIX

The Intersection of Medicine, Ethics, and Society

Historical Echoes: The Lobotomy and Gender Transition Procedures

Examining the annals of medical history, it is evident that the field has frequently wrestled with ethically complex procedures and treatments. For instance, in the mid-20th century, the lobotomy was seen as a revolutionary treatment for a variety of mental health conditions (El-Hai, 2005). As contemporary research has revealed, this method was critically flawed and harmful, often leaving patients with permanent damage (Diefenbach et al., 1999). Today, we reflect on this somber period in medical history with astonishment and disbelief, questioning how such a brutal procedure could have been considered acceptable (Pressman, 1998).

Now, in the present day, we face another challenging medical landscape: gender reassignment procedures. The comparison is not to say that they are identical or equivalent, but to

reflect on how they are both radical medical interventions addressing complex mental and psychological conditions. Gender reassignment surgery, however, differs fundamentally from lobotomy in its purpose and ethical framework. It aims to alleviate gender dysphoria by aligning the physical body with an individual's internal gender identity, purportedly providing substantial relief and improved quality of life for many transgender individuals, though the body of research on the matter is not yet sufficient to suggest this with any degree of certainty.

However, the comparison poses an intriguing perspective: Are we currently overlooking potential issues in our enthusiastic endorsement of these procedures, just as many were blind to the harms of lobotomy in its time? Are we too readily accepting the idea that the physical body is at fault when an individual's mental self-perception doesn't align with their biological sex?

To illustrate, imagine if the dysphoria was not about gender, but about species or age. Would we readily accept and affirm those perceptions as objective reality, urging for medical procedures to align the body with these self-perceptions? Where do we draw the line and based on what principles?

It's vital to make it clear that this argument does not imply that gender transition procedures are fundamentally harmful or negative, much like lobotomies. Instead, it invites a reflective and open dialogue on our understanding of gender dysphoria and our response to it. Are we, in an effort to affirm individual self-perception, perhaps overstepping the bounds of reasonable medical intervention? Are we hastily labeling the

body as "wrong" instead of exploring other avenues of understanding and managing gender dysphoria?

These are challenging questions, and they reflect the ongoing struggle within medicine and society to balance empathy and affirmation with critical inquiry and measured judgment. In the end, it serves as a reminder that our understanding of human identity and health is constantly evolving, and so too should our approaches to addressing complex human conditions.

Mass Sociogenic Illness, the Placebo Effect, and American Society: A Complex Tapestry of Mind and Culture

Mass sociogenic illness, also known as mass psychogenic illness, is a fascinating phenomenon where a group of individuals collectively manifest physical symptoms that have no identifiable physical cause, typically triggered by stress or anxiety. The placebo effect, on the other hand, is the phenomenon where a patient experiences a perceived improvement in their condition due solely to their belief in the efficacy of a treatment, regardless of whether the treatment has any therapeutic value.

Although seemingly distinct, these phenomena both highlight the extraordinary power of the mind and belief, and how our psychological state can influence our physical well-being. In both cases, it's the individuals' belief—whether in a

perceived threat or in the efficacy of a treatment—that leads to physical manifestations.

Strange Contagion by Lee Daniel Kravetz offers a deep-dive into the social contagion phenomenon, particularly focusing on a series of suicides in Palo Alto, California. Through a thorough investigation, Kravetz observes that the community seemed to be caught in a distressing cycle of self-harm, which he links to the concept of social contagion. This is the idea that behaviors, emotions, and ideas can spread through populations much like infectious diseases. Drawing upon a wealth of research, he explains that certain behaviors can ripple through communities, influencing others to think and act in similar ways. This ripple effect was particularly pronounced in the high-pressure, achievement-oriented environment of Palo Alto, where stress, anxiety, and feelings of inadequacy were pervasive.

The "June bug" incident referenced in Bartholomew and Wessely's "Protean nature of mass sociogenic illness" is another compelling case study in this context. In 1962, a North Carolina textile mill was swept by an outbreak of mysterious symptoms, ranging from dizziness and nausea to fainting. The epidemic, attributed to a bug bite, affected 62 workers, predominantly women. However, medical and entomological investigations found no evidence of any insect responsible for the outbreak. Instead, the authors point out that the outbreak's symptoms were likely induced by psychological factors, particularly the stressful, monotonous working conditions and tight social network within the mill. The "June bug" epidemic exemplifies how social and psychological factors can

manifest in physical symptoms, a key feature of mass sociogenic illness.

Both instances underscore the power of social influence in shaping individual and collective behaviors, emotions, and even physical health. The concept of social contagion challenges the commonly held view of individuals as solely autonomous agents, instead painting a picture of deeply interconnected beings whose thoughts, feelings, and behaviors are continually shaped by their social environments. Whether in a high-pressure school environment or a stressful workplace, social contagion can amplify stress, fear, and even harmful behaviors, underscoring the need for interventions that address the social and psychological dimensions of health and well-being. The "June bug" incident further expands our understanding of the body-mind connection, illustrating how emotional distress can manifest in physical symptoms, a phenomenon that continues to be an important area of research in modern psychology and medicine.

In the American context, sociocultural factors, such as media influence, play a significant role in both mass sociogenic illness and the placebo effect. A 2019 study published in the *Journal of Clinical Psychology* titled "Media and mass hysteria: A case study analysis," explores how media reporting can trigger or exacerbate mass hysteria. Similarly, media and advertising significantly impact the placebo effect, shaping consumer expectations about the effectiveness of a range of products, from pharmaceuticals to cosmetics.

These phenomena can also be seen in the context of American society's emphasis on health and wellness. In a

culture that places a high value on physical health and appearance, the fear of being unwell can lead to manifestations of mass sociogenic illness. On the other hand, the faith in modern medicine and treatments can enhance the placebo effect.

Understanding these phenomena is crucial as they provide insight into the intersection of psychology, society, and culture. They underscore the importance of considering the psychological and sociocultural factors when addressing health and wellness issues in society and remind us of the power of the mind in shaping our physical reality.

CHAPTER THIRTY-ONE

Émile Coué:
Optimistic Autosuggestion

Researchers in the mental health field have explored how we can harness the placebo effect and the innate suggestibility of the human psyche for positive outcomes. Émile Coué was a French psychologist and pharmacist who introduced a popular method of psychotherapy and self-improvement based on optimistic autosuggestion, known as the Coué method.

His most famous affirmation is: "Every day, in every way, I am getting better and better." He believed that repeating this phrase multiple times a day could improve one's condition. Coué posited that any imagined malady or problem could be cured or improved through his method of optimistic self-suggestion.

His work was built on the premise that any idea exclusively occupying the mind turns into reality, although only to the extent that the idea is within the realm of possibility. He emphasized that his method did not rely on hypnosis but rather on

the power of suggestion and the belief that the subconscious mind was a potent force that could be directed to produce positive outcomes.

As we have already explored in previous sections, the mind is capable of astounding feats of accomplishment, even without our conscious sense of awareness towards what is transpiring. So, at this moment, we are going to repeat the affirmation. Think of this like a guided mantra meditation. Imagine I am repeating it along with you. Just be sure to not stop until we get to the end of the section. Here we go:

The Mantra-

Every day, in every way, I am getting better and better. Every day, in every way, I am getting better and better. Every day, in every way, I am getting better and better. Every day, in every way, I am getting better and better. Every day, in every way, I am getting better and better. Every day, in every way, I am getting better and better. Every day, in every way, I am getting better and better. Every day, in every way, I am getting better and better. Every day, in every way, I am getting better and better. Every day, in every way, I am getting better and better. Every day, in every way, I am getting better and better. Every day, in every way, I am getting better and better. Every day, in every way, I am getting better and better. Every day, in every way, I am getting better and better. Every day, in every way, I am getting better and better. Every day, in every way, I am getting better and better. Every day, in every way, I am getting better and better. Every day, in every way, I am getting better and better. Every day, in every way, I am getting better and better. Every day, in every way, I am getting better and

better. Every day, in every way, I am getting better and better. Every day, in every way, I am getting better and better. Every day, in every way, I am getting better and better. Every day, in every way, I am getting better and better.

Every day, in every way, I am getting better and better. Every day, in every way, I am getting better and better.

Every day, in every way, I am getting better and better. Every day, in every way, I am getting better and better. Every day, in every way, I am getting better and better. Every day, in

every way, I am getting better and better. Every day, in every way, I am

getting better and better. Every day, in every way, I am getting better and better. Every day, in every way, I am getting better and better. Every day, in every way, I am getting better and better. Every day, in every way, I am getting better and better. Every day, in every way, I am getting better and better. Every day, in every way, I am getting better and better. Every day, in every way, I am getting better and better. Every day, in every way, I am getting better and better. Every day, in every way, I am getting better and better. Every day, in every way, I am getting better and better. Every day, in every way, I am getting better and better. Every day, in every way, I am getting better and better. Every day, in every way, I am getting better and better. Every day, in every way, I am getting better and better. Every day, in every way, I am getting better and better.

Every day, in every way, I am getting better and better. Every day, in every way, I am getting better and better. Every day, in every way, I am getting better and better. Every day, in every way, I am getting better and better. Every day, in every way, I am getting better and better. Every day, in every way, I am getting better and better. Every day, in every way, I am getting better and better. Every day, in every way, I am getting better and better. Every day, in every way, I am getting better and better. Every day, in every way, I am getting better and better. Every day, in every way, I am getting better and better. Every day, in every way, I am getting better and better. Every day, in every way, I am getting better and better. Every day, in every way, I am getting better and better. Every day, in every way, I am getting better and better. Every day, in every way, I am getting better and better. Every day, in every way, I am getting better and better. Every day, in every way, I am getting better and better. Every day, in every way, I am getting better

and better. Every day, in every way, I am getting better and better. Every day, in every way, I am getting better and better. Every day, in every way, I am getting better and better. Every day, in every way, I am getting better and better. Every day, in every way, I am getting better and better. Every day, in every way, I am getting better and better. Every day, in every way, I am getting better and better. Every day, in every way, I am getting better and better. Every day, in every way, I am getting better and better. Every day, in every way, I am getting better and better. Every day, in every way, I am getting better and better. Every day, in every way, I am getting better and better. Every day, in every way, I am getting better and better.

Every day, in every way, I am getting better and better. Every day, in every way, I am getting better and better. Every day, in every way, I am getting better and better. Every day, in every way, I am getting better and better. Every day, in every way, I am getting better and better. Every day, in every way, I am getting better and better. Every day, in every way, I am getting better and better. Every day, in every way, I am getting better and better. Every day, in every way, I am getting better and better. Every day, in every way, I am getting better and better. Every day, in every way, I am getting better and better. Every day, in every way, I am getting better and better. Every day, in every way, I am getting better and better. Every day, in every way, I am getting better and better. Every day, in every way, I am getting better and better. Every day, in every way, I am getting better and better. Every day, in every way, I am getting better and better. Every day, in every way, I am getting better and better. Every day, in every way, I am getting better and better. Every day, in every way, I am getting better and better.

Every day, in every way, I am getting better and better. Every day, in every way, I am getting better and better.

Keep coming back to this section every day, repeating the mantra, and see if it has any quantifiable benefit to your daily life. Try it in different mindsets and physical environments. Perhaps there's a specific arrangement of parameters most conducive to your particular experience of effective autosuggestion.

CHAPTER THIRTY-TWO

Perception, Validation, and Hope in Mental Health Care

Therapists often artfully engage in conversations that appear to impart deep insights into an individual's character while offering tools to address trauma adaptations. However, this approach largely depends on self-reporting and uses psychological constructs that, in many cases, haven't undergone a comprehensive validation process — one that ensures their reliability, accuracy, and utility across different contexts and populations. Contrary to popular belief, mainstream psychology, driven by an abstractionist ontology, often assumes that theories and principles inherently embody the truth. This approach overlooks the idea that practices are deeply rooted in specific situations and cultures, suggesting a relational ontology. Such a relational perspective, which emphasizes the interdependence of concepts and their contexts, challenges the manual-driven approach in psychology and demands a more nuanced understanding of therapeutic practices. (Slife, 2004). Understanding these theoretical

perspectives provides a backdrop against which we can better appreciate the practical challenges and dynamics present in therapist-client interactions.

After the evaluation period with a new practitioner, the fundamental value of the therapeutic process often hinges on the counselor's ability to meaningfully engage with the client, a dynamic that remains essential even within the confines of standardized treatment. Specifically, therapists with a high degree of relatability or empathy, tend to achieve better outcomes and stronger therapeutic alliances. Conversely, low-empathy or confrontational approaches often result in higher drop-out and relapse rates, signifying the crucial role of emotional connection in the therapeutic relationship. (Moyers & Miller, 2013). There are concerns about the efficacy of therapy overall, suggesting a shift towards more objective, evidence-based practices. However, the term "evidence-based therapy" often refers to manualized therapies (standardized treatment approaches), notably cognitive behavior therapy variants. Despite claims of their superiority, research has not definitively proven them more effective than other psychotherapies. Many patients don't achieve lasting benefits, and the actual advantages of these therapies might be overstated due to questionable research practices. (Shedler, 2018).

The global mental health system frequently fails many individuals due to its inherent subjectivity—a significant obstacle that arises from the varying perceptions held by patients and therapists alike. The pursuit of therapy or medication typically requires personal initiative, but when these interventions fail, the reasons may not be clear (Gaudiano, Beevers, &

Miller, 2011). Is it a failure in the pharmacological approach, inadequacy of the practitioner, or just faulty self-reporting? This ambiguity often makes it equally uncertain what alternative strategies might be more effective. Individuals may seek out therapists who they can identify with based on demography or shared personal experience, as this would increase the likelihood of being understood beyond the semantics of language. But this is not guaranteed, as therapists tend to conform to a relatively narrow range of demographic characteristics, with a majority percentage being white and female (American Psychological Association, 2015).

The result is a seemingly arbitrary cycle of trial and error, devoid of an objective pathway to solve perceived problems. In this scenario, the efficacy of a treatment is often determined solely based on its subjective "feel" potentially being attributed to the placebo effect (Howick et al., 2013). However, this approach is inherently flawed because it can lead to misguided perceptions of the core issue. As mentioned, cognitive behavioral therapy proves to be an effective alternative for some, but it is not a perfect solution either.

Assuming the individual seeking help isn't delusional and reaches a point of despair due to unsuccessful mental health solutions, they may become mired in hopelessness. Persistently trying various options with dwindling faith in their efficacy can be demoralizing. Once the threshold of hopelessness is crossed, it's not uncommon for individuals to abandon their efforts altogether.

Subsequently, society may unfairly critique these individuals for not "trying hard enough," resulting in a profound sense

of shame over circumstances beyond their control. Such experiences of isolation and lack of solutions to a perceived crisis inevitably fuel despondency. Ultimately, the stigma associated with mental health issues and the futile exertion of effort in the face of such desolation can evoke a profound sense of frustration, and potentially increase suicidality (Rüsch et al., 2014).

As discussed elsewhere in this book, and hopefully facilitated by the information contained herein, there are numerous ways to try to attain peace or stability within our lives without specifically hitching our wagon to unreliable or uncertain externalities. I would hope that this overarching sequence of words can find the right placement within one's intellect and potentially prompt some sort of qualitatively beneficial limbic response. And, by my own nature, I would be inclined to say, "reach out to me if you need to talk things out," but clearly that wouldn't be the long-term solution for anyone with deep-seated psychological issues or a complete deficit in social support. It may seem paradoxical, but sometimes, there's solace in acknowledging the finality of certain situations. If it truly feels like there's no turning back, if bridges have been burned, or if chances have been missed, then dwelling on the past serves little purpose. We'll delve deeper into this concept later, but it felt pertinent to touch upon it now.

Take a Break

Now might be a good time for a little cognitive "breather" to help refresh and refocus our thoughts. Let's take a moment to stare at a blank surface, reflecting on everything that has been said thus far, or perhaps on what remains unspoken. Alternatively, feel free to think of absolutely nothing. Simply allow the mind to achieve a momentary "tabula rasa" by focusing on something devoid of information and grounding yourself within the present state of your external existence wherever that may be. Feel free to use the next three pages for this exercise, if there is too much stimulus in your current environment.

Illuminating Unconventional Wisdom

CHAPTER THIRTY-THREE

An Illumination of Unconventional Brilliance

Terry A. Davis was a figure of profound intellect and unconventional creativity. His life and philosophy, though marked by personal struggles, showcased an astounding dedication to a unique vision and an exceptional mastery of technological craft. His singular vision was evident in his creation of TempleOS, an operating system he built from scratch, along with its own version of the C programming language fittingly labeled HolyC. This project serves as a testament to his technical proficiency, boundless imagination, and his commitment to seeing his vision through, despite its divergence from mainstream expectations. What makes TempleOS particularly remarkable is that it is a 16-bit, non-networked operating system, reminiscent of the early days of personal computing. The retro aesthetic, combined with the complexity of the coding required to bring it to life, demonstrates a deep understanding of and respect for the foundations of computing.

In this endeavor, Davis embodied the essence of the "lone genius" archetype, devoting himself to a project that was deeply personal and uniquely his. In a technological world marked by homogeneity, his work stands as an emblem of personal authenticity and conviction. His philosophical viewpoint mirrored this authenticity, as his work served as a means to convey his sincere sense of spirituality, and TempleOS itself serving as a sort of platform for others to congregate and experience the divine, describing the operating system as "God's official temple. Just like Solomon's temple, this is a community focal point where offerings are made and God's oracle is consulted." To Davis, coding was a deeply spiritual act, one that linked the individual, the machine, and the divine in an act of creation (Hicks, 2014).

Despite the challenges he faced, not least of which being his schizophrenic mental state—the sort of general malaise only the genius possesses and the insane lament—Davis' life and philosophy inspire on multiple levels. They serve as a reminder of the power of single-minded dedication to a vision, of the beauty that can arise from the fusion of technology and spirituality, and of the inherent worth of pursuing a path that is authentically one's own. His legacy, encapsulated in his unique creation, continues to intrigue and inspire.

Perhaps Davis intrinsically understood something that few could ever know. Venturing into the realm of Gnosticism, one is met with a realm of knowledge reserved for the enlightened few, an esoteric belief system that embodies the pursuit of divine wisdom. At its core, Gnosticism grapples with the spiritual understanding of the world, the cosmos, and the

divine essence, proffering a grandeur vision of mankind's destiny that surpasses the mundane sphere.

Within the compendium of computing, we direct our attention toward the field of mathematics, and here the conceptual journey transitions from metaphysical landscapes to the firmament of logic and reasoning. Mathematical axioms, the foundation of the edifice of mathematics, are accepted as self-evident truths, the bedrock upon which the towering structures of mathematical theories and constructs rise.

Now, on first glance, these two spheres—Gnosticism and mathematical axioms—might appear distant, divergent even. But let's explore these potential interconnections. The subtle frequencies of a profound resonance can be heard between the intrinsic and the extrinsic, the divine and the logical, and the known and the unknowable. Gnosticism, a yearning for divine knowledge, is akin to a mathematician's quest for an elusive proof. A pursuit that often flirts with the realm of the unknown, the unproven. The Gnostic seeks illumination through a mystical understanding of the divine, an intuitive and introspective quest, much like a mathematician's introspection on axioms, those self-evident truths from which all else flows. Much like a mathematical axiom, the Gnostic knowledge, once attained, is experienced as self-evident, an incontrovertible truth that resonates deep within the enlightened soul. The common thread that ties these two realms together, however disparate they might seem, is the essence of belief—belief in the self-evident truth, belief in the unseen and intangible, belief in the profound connection that binds us all to the cosmos and the divine. Hence, this exploration

reveals an intriguing symbiosis: Gnosticism and mathematical axioms, though superficially different, are bound by the pursuit of knowledge and understanding, the ceaseless human quest to make sense of the world and the cosmos. Both, in their unique ways, embody the aspiration to comprehend the very fabric of existence.

Weaving from the threads of Gnosticism and mathematical axioms, we find ourselves at the doorstep of a profound concept: axiomatic truth. This is the fundamental principle that posits certain propositions as self-evident. Herein, the foundation of mathematical logic is laid, birthing an elegant edifice of truth-structures that carry the weight of countless theorems. Yet, as firm as this foundation appears, it does bear the scars of paradox, an echo of humanity's perpetual struggle with the infinite and the undefined. Among these, Russell's paradox stands tall, a reminder that even within the rigorous confines of logic and axiomatic truth, contradictions may sprout, casting long shadows of doubt over our mathematical edifices.

Russell's paradox, discovered by the philosopher and logician Bertrand Russell, is a fascinating instance of self-reference and self-contradiction within set theory, an area of mathematics concerned with the properties of well-defined collections of objects. It grapples with the question: does the set of all sets that do not contain themselves include itself? The paradox lies in the contradiction that if it does, then by definition it shouldn't, and if it doesn't, then by definition, it should. This paradox reveals a crack in the axiomatic truth system, casting a net of intrigue over the mathematical landscape. The

paradox suggests that our foundational understanding of sets, themselves fundamental to mathematical axioms, is incomplete, or that our logic is somehow inconsistent. But herein lies a striking symmetry with the path of Gnosticism. Just as the enlightened Gnostic learns to embrace the divine mystery, so too must the mathematician make peace with the paradoxical. Both Gnosticism and the pursuit of axiomatic truth ask of us to dwell comfortably in the space of the unknowable, to recognize the borders of human understanding and see the beauty within those borders. Hence, Russell's Paradox, rather than casting a shadow on our pursuit of truth, illuminates the labyrinthine beauty of the logical world and the delightful complexity of our quest for understanding. Even within the rigorous logic of mathematics, we find echoes of the mystical, the enigmatic, and the divine.

Transitioning into the psychological landscape of Carl Jung, we find an analogous concept to the paradoxical contradictions within axiomatic systems: the shadow. Jung's shadow represents the unconscious aspects of the personality, the parts of ourselves that we don't acknowledge or even realize exist. It's the repository for our fears, repressed desires, and elements deemed socially unacceptable. It is the part of ourselves that is not known, and often not wanted. And yet, it is an integral part of our personality, as much a part of us as the aspects we readily acknowledge.

The Jungian shadow mirrors the paradox we've encountered in mathematics. Just as Russell's paradox exposes the inherent contradictions within a seemingly consistent and clear logical system, the shadow symbolizes the inherent

contradictions within the self. It's the embodiment of the tension between the known and the unknown, the acknowledged and the unacknowledged. It is both part of us and alien to us, a self-contradiction similar to the one Russell uncovered in set theory. Moreover, both Russell's paradox and the shadow underline the necessity of embracing the inherent contradictions within our systems of understanding. In both cases, it's only through acknowledging these paradoxes that we can progress towards greater self-awareness and understanding. Jung encouraged individuals to confront and integrate their shadows into their conscious personality—to confront the paradox within. Similarly, mathematicians don't abandon their pursuit of knowledge because of Russell's paradox but instead use it to refine the foundations of mathematical logic.

Thus, we see a profound parallel between our mathematical, psychological, and even artistic journeys. Both Russell's paradox and the Jungian shadow, as well as the enigmatic creativity of Terry Davis, serve as illuminating torches, guiding us to embrace the ambiguity and contradictions that accompany the quest for understanding and self-realization. They invite us to delve into the realms of the not-yet-known, enriching our exploration of the world and ourselves, and reminding us that one man's genius is another man's madness. It's all about perspective. We'll explore another manifestation of perspective in the next section.

CHAPTER THIRTY-FOUR

Birth of Brilliance: Unraveling the Mysteries of the Creative Process

Often, "brilliance" in filmmaking is synonymous with being a "visionary." Simply put, you either possess an "eye for it" or you don't. Renowned and unknown film directors alike harbor the misconception that complex, high-tech equipment and distinctive locations are prerequisites for effective storytelling or the realization of their artistic visions. However, the annals of the moving picture industry bear numerous instances of celebrated artists who have successfully challenged this belief. Directors such as Christopher Nolan and Quentin Tarantino have showcased their prowess by creating compelling feature debuts that thrive on minimalistic location settings and modest production value, while uncompromising the emphasis on classic elements of filmmaking. In situations where particular creative elements could not be captured within the budgetary constraints, the framing of the film implies that these events

occurred off screen (e.g., *Reservoir Dogs* showing the audience the aftermath of the heist, while omitting the inciting incident.)

Another case in point: filmmakers like Andrew Bujalski and the Duplass Brothers, pioneers of the "mumblecore" movement in the early 2000s, have achieved critical acclaim by leveraging extremely limited resources available to them, in order to build the foundation of their film legacy. This innovative genre is characterized by its heavy reliance on improvisation, naturalistic settings, negligible or absent scripting, and the use of whatever practical locations and affordable camera equipment that could be mustered. The cornerstone of these "mumblecore" films is their emphasis on the profundity of character interaction and dialogue, which resounds clearly regardless of the application of conventional filmmaking techniques. These filmmakers demonstrate that the essence of a story transcends the trappings of high-end production, and that a compelling narrative can be crafted from simplicity and authenticity.

Directors like Mark Phillips expand this concept further. His comedy group catapulted to success as influencers and content creators by crafting sketch comedy videos in their own home, completely eschewing set dressing or special props. Whether the script called for a locker room or a fantasy setting, the production design remained localized in their unset-dressed living room or local park, with no attempts to mimic the intended setting. Their triumph underscores the power of audience imagination; if the acting is captivating and

the dialogue engaging, viewers are more than willing to fill in the environmental gaps themselves.

Comedy, with its inherent absurdities and exaggerations, may lend itself more readily to such rudimentary DIY production methods. However, this truth applies across all mediums and genres, and spans the full scope of the human experience. When an individual's authenticity shines through in their passion and interest, the audience, or community at large, senses it and engagement deepens. This truth has been borne out historically, even in cases where creators intended their work to provoke or deride their audience.

Consider Luis Buñuel's *Un Chien Andalou*, created with the express aim of affronting the bourgeoisie intelligentsia Buñuel had encountered at university. Despite its intentions, or perhaps because of them, the film was embraced by the very demographic it sought to insult, launching Buñuel's filmmaking career. Salvador Dali's status at the time may have contributed to the film's success, but the essence remains the same: even a surrealist insult can find its niche in the market ecosystem if it resonates with an authentic space within the creator.

The key takeaway here is that authenticity and sincere passion, combined with engaging performances and dialogue, can often supersede the need for elaborate settings, props, or high-end production value. This insight holds great promise for aspiring artists and creators operating with limited resources, suggesting that the route to success may not be as inaccessible as it often appears.

Stewart Copeland, a renowned drummer from The Police, serves as a prime exemplar of the profound concept that

unique creative expressions are more deeply ingrained in the innateness of one's personality and physiology rather than being contingent upon optimal external conditions. Even when playing on a severely compromised, out-of-tune drum kit, Copeland's distinctive sound is unmistakable, thus reinforcing this view. His onetime bandmate Les Claypool has attested to this fact on record in an interview session a few years ago (https://youtu.be/aPNmqNtZi20).

Such instances underline the fundamental truth that creativity emanates from a place of authenticity and sincerity. Once the rudimentary level of technical prowess is achieved—an attainment within the reach of most individuals with typical physical capabilities—the ensuing display of talent stems from a person's abstract characteristics and abilities.

Here, it is important to distinguish between the mastery of technical skills and the expression of unique, innate creativity. The former can be taught, learned, and improved upon through deliberate practice and effort. The latter, however, is more elusive and intangible—it is an extension of one's unique personality and life experiences. It is this intrinsic creativity, emanating from the innermost depths of a person's being, that allows artists like Copeland to create unique and memorable artistic expressions, regardless of the external circumstances.

The remarkable journey of the band Alice in Chains, during the production of their critically acclaimed EP *Jar of Flies*, serves as an intriguing illustration of overcoming perceived obstacles to achieve goals. The EP, birthed in a backdrop of housing eviction and subsequent studio-dwelling, with the

added transition of a new band member, Mike Inez, under-scores the resilience of human creativity amidst adversity.

Such narratives compel one to reflect on the prevailing perception of impediments as insurmountable barriers. Considering Inez's experience—transitioning from playing bass for Ozzy Osbourne to joining a band navigating a turbulent period—one could hardly find any indication of the chaotic circumstances hindering their creative process. Paradoxically, perhaps, these challenging circumstances appear to have fueled their creative direction, inspiring the band to opt for a comparatively somber, acoustic approach when contrasted with the group's earlier work. This story underscores a significant insight: the actualization of one's goals will invariably materialize when the vision and conviction—the components of what some radical thinkers call the "power process"—are present. It's not so much a choice as it is a mathematical certainty. If we accept this, we can draw a corollary that stagnation, a lack of progress or goal achievement, suggests the absence of these requisite elements. Consequently, life, in its ebb and flow, is precisely as it should be.

Our place in society sets in motion our internal impeller, eliciting a sense of purpose, a drive to do something or go somewhere. Absent this anchorage, we risk being aimlessly carried by life's currents. The anchoring force of the power process allows us to stay rooted and enables the transformation of abstract concepts into tangible outcomes, effectively steering us through life's currents towards our ultimate destination.

In essence, we are integral parts of an interconnected cos-mic tapestry—the quantum field vibrations, the energy flows, the causal trajectory—they all move within and around us. We perceive these dynamics from an egocentric perspective, but in reality, we also serve as conduits of flow for others. When we achieve our goals, it reflects another interaction in the field, the outcome of which can be quantified and appreciated.

Unpacking the Hidden Impacts of the Customer Service Paradigm

The mantra "the customer is always right" is deeply ingrained in American culture, dictating our norms and expectations within the marketplace. However, beneath the seemingly benign customer-centric facade, this model can inadvertently perpetuate power hierarchies, creating conditions that are exploitative and unjust. In its essence, this slogan suggests an unequal power dynamic where the customer possesses ultimate authority. While initially intended to encourage high standards of service, the mantra has been interpreted by some to grant customers unbounded entitlement. This may foster a toxic environment where employees or service providers are forced to tolerate unreasonable demands or behaviors under the threat of job insecurity or financial instability.

Moreover, this model propagates a scarcity mindset, where service providers, particularly independent contractors, often accept unfavorable deals for fear of missing out on future opportunities or because they feel there's no alternative. This fear, often exacerbated by economic uncertainties, can lead to a pattern of accepting unfair conditions, thus reinforcing an unhealthy power dynamic. This unbalanced dynamic also impacts individuals further down the business hierarchy. As each level of management or subcontracting distances an individual from the core decision-making, the stress associated with this uncertainty intensifies, often resulting in anxiety and job dissatisfaction.

Beyond the immediate professional implications, the relentless adherence to the "customer is always right" principle exacts a significant emotional toll on service providers. Over time, being constantly positioned as the "lesser" in an interaction can erode self-worth and diminish one's self-respect. Employees may begin to internalize negative feedback, conflating their value as professionals with their ability to appease even the most unreasonable of customers. This can lead to burnout, mental health issues, and decreased job satisfaction. Furthermore, the boundary between personal and professional life can blur. The constant need to placate and appease can make it challenging for service providers to assert themselves in personal relationships and settings. They may find themselves struggling to set boundaries or advocate for their needs, having been conditioned to prioritize others' desires over their own. The solution lies not just in businesses reevaluating their service protocols but also in empowering employees with training and support that allow them to assert boundaries,

manage stress, and differentiate between constructive feedback and undue criticism. Equipping our workforce with these tools is crucial if we hope to reverse the harmful effects of this deeply entrenched ideology.

And just as the concept of the engagement ring, a product of clever marketing, became rooted in our cultural understanding of courtship, so too has the "customer is always right" ideology seeped into our collective consciousness. It has shaped our expectations not only of service but also of power dynamics within professional and romantic relationships.

In order to counter these negative impacts, we must first acknowledge the underlying issues. We must challenge the narratives that perpetuate exploitative power dynamics and advocate for business models that prioritize respect, fairness, and equitable treatment for all involved. Recognizing the human element in business interactions is the first step towards creating a more balanced, just, and ultimately successful marketplace.

Exploring Complex Ideas

Exploring Societal Dynamics Through the Lens of Astrophysics and Quantum Physics

Observations from cosmology indicate that the universe is in a state of perpetual expansion, driven by the pervasive and enigmatic forces of dark matter and dark energy. This cosmic expansion can be likened to the growth and diversification of human civilization, which continually spreads and evolves as populations increase and more people come into existence, causing societal structures to balloon and sprawl across the globe.

As a parallel, consider the Doppler effect, where a light source moving relative to an observer experiences a shift in its color spectrum. As a light source recedes from us, its light appears more red (a redshift), while it appears more blue as it approaches us (a blueshift). This effect is commonly observed

in astrophysics, but could also offer a metaphor for the shifting ideologies in society. Ideologies, much like light, are forms of energy that take substantial shape when interacted with or observed. Thus, as society grows and evolves, the perceived hue of an ideology may shift depending on the observer's position, even while its fundamental energy remains consistent. For instance, perceived shifts in the American political spectrum, from "red" to "blue" and vice versa, could be seen as an ideological Doppler effect, depending on the relative position of the voter.

Exploring further parallels with quantum physics, the concept of conservation of mass and energy suggests that knowledge—like mass and energy—is neither created nor destroyed. This principle implies that the sum total of all conceivable knowledge has been present since the universe's inception, becoming progressively more accessible to humans through scientific developments and the creation of lasting, transferable media. Essentially, we "divine" our knowledge from the ether, as epistemological prophets, interpreting the cosmic will through our material rituals and experiments, then storing the information on disk drives, like a modern-age Ark of the Covenant. Every visual manifestation that we create from this perception of divinity serves as an idol or tribute to the invisible.

The saying "a picture is worth a thousand words" highlights the immense amount of information an image can convey and its potential to inspire thought or action. With future technological advancements, we could discover innovative ways to convey information, possibly shifting from speech to

solely using visual data, and once we exceed the biological limits for our human expressions, we may open new dimensions of communication within the measurable knowledge spectrum.

However, akin to the concept of dark matter and dark energy, there might exist an analogous "dark knowledge" that pervades the realm of ignorance. Though it is unmeasurable and practically unusable, it might still exert influence on our universe, much like dark matter influences the cosmic fabric. This speculative analogy could potentially offer a metaphorical explanation for some of the challenging phenomena observed in global society today. As we delve deeper into our understanding of the universe, we realize that much like the cosmos is vast and largely unexplored, human cognition too harbors vast untapped potentials. Just as astronomers and physicists look beyond the visible spectrum to uncover the secrets of the universe, perhaps we should expand our epistemological methods, venturing beyond the known paradigms of knowledge acquisition. By embracing new methodologies and interdisciplinary approaches, we might be able to tap into this 'dark knowledge,' bridging the gap between the known and the unknown, the seen and the unseen. Such a pursuit not only has the potential to elevate our collective consciousness but also to unlock untapped avenues of innovation and progression, ensuring that humanity remains in sync with the ever-evolving tapestry of the cosmos.

Causality, Free Will, and the Infinite Library

Engaging with the eternal discourse on free will, we find ourselves inevitably navigating the complex corridors of causality. The dichotomy of free will versus determinism mirrors Conway's Game of Life, where the inherent rules of the game dictate the future state of each cell based on its initial configuration (Gardner, 1970).

This cellular automaton becomes a powerful metaphor for life itself, suggesting that the "seeds" of our initial conditions—our circumstances, genetics, and experiences - interact within the confines of deterministic rules to create the unique pattern of our existence. It suggests that the totality of our lives, our triumphs, our failures, and even our most profound thoughts are but predetermined echoes of these initial seeds.

However, just as the game's outcome can dramatically shift with the slightest alteration to the starting configuration, our lives can be profoundly transformed by seemingly

inconsequential choices. Herein lies the debate: is this exercise of choice merely an illusion, a predetermined interaction of the initial seeds, or a manifestation of free will?

Within this realm of contemplation, it's worth reflecting on the groundbreaking experiments of Benjamin Libet. Venturing into the intricacies of neuroscience behind our decision-making process, Libet's work in the 1980s aimed to discern the relationship between conscious intention and neurological activity. He proposed that our brains might initiate decisions before we're consciously aware of them. Through his studies, participants carried out simple motor tasks, noting the precise moment they felt the conscious urge to act. Interestingly, the electroencephalogram (EEG) readings showed that the brain's preparatory activity began milliseconds before the participants' conscious decision. This discovery suggests that our choices might be established in our neural pathways before our conscious self becomes aware, adding another layer to the intricate interplay between choice, determinism, and free will in the sociological landscape.

Sam Harris, renowned neuroscientist and philosopher, delved deeper into the interplay between brain activity and choice. Working in collaboration with a team of researchers, Harris expanded upon the foundational work of Libet by harnessing the advancements in modern neuroimaging techniques, using functional magnetic resonance imaging (fMRI) to investigate the neural roots of decision-making. In the study, participants made a binary choice and indicated their awareness of the decision. The results, showing that brain

activity anticipated conscious choice, confirmed Libet's earlier discoveries.

Approaching the notion in terms of abstract causality, Jorge Luis Borges' *The Library of Babel* offers an intriguing perspective (Borges, 1941). This hypothetical library, containing every possible permutation of words and letters, posits a universe where every thought, every idea, and every literary work is already etched into the fabric of existence.

Eight decades after the publication of "The Library of Babel," we've entered an era where Borges' imaginative vision has been given form through modern technology. Computer scientist and author Jonathan Basile has taken the abstract concept and operationalized it algorithmically on his website, Library of Babel. The site employs an algorithm that generates 'books,' each comprised of every permutation of 29 characters, including the 26 English letters, a space, a comma, and a period. Users can navigate this virtual hexagonal library via coordinates, ensuring they can always locate the same 'book' in the same place. With the ability to generate all possible pages of 3,200 characters, the website offers access to an astounding 10^{4677} potential pages. Both Borges' narrative and its digital adaptation reveal a fundamental aspect of language's nature. Although the prevalent belief is that language derives its meaning from the conscious intent of the speaker or writer, the Library of Babel contests this idea, serving as a critique of traditional semantics and Saussure's theories. It suggests that language can exist even without any intent to signify meaning. In this context, every utterance we make, no matter how heartfelt or impromptu, becomes indistinguishable from its

mechanical repetition. Upon revisiting Saussure's framework of the link between the signifier and the signified, it becomes possible to extract meaning from the abstract, converting what is generally dismissed as meaningless babble—as much of the Library of Babel most certainly is—into something with intent. This could be seen as a transition from Dadaist chaos to Realist clarity. Though I suppose that wouldn't be very Dada in nature.

Anyway, back to the core premise of this section. Through this algorithmic conceptualization, the emergence of an idea becomes akin to uncovering a specific book from the library. Each thought, each idea, seems less an act of creation and more an act of discovery—drawing into question the role of free will. Are we but vessels channeling the algorithmic ether of the cosmos, or architects sculpting the landscape of our ideas?

To truly engage with the philosophical implications of these models, we must reconcile the dichotomy of free will and causality. We are both products of our initial conditions and participants in the unfolding pattern of our lives. The balance between these forces forms the symphony of existence, with each note a testament to the intricacies between the predetermined, and the freely chosen. In short, you are the captain and vessel of your own experience, and will be held accountable regardless.

CHAPTER THIRTY-EIGHT

Causality, Determinism, and Human Agency: The Cosmic Procession of Action and Consequence

In the continuous interplay of action and consequence, timing often takes center stage. The advice to "just start," regardless of timing, underscores our limited sway amidst countless uncontrollable variables. This sentiment emphasizes the deterministic forces that shape outcomes, from initiating a new project to exploring a hobby.

From the deterministic perspective, each decision or action isn't merely a product of free will but emerges from a chain of preceding causes. Like a series of dominoes, each event influences the next, all the way back to the universe's dawn—the Big Bang. Such consistent cause-and-effect is what defines determinism.

Through this lens, even our motivations appear sculpted by deterministic waves. When we opt to embark on an endeavor, it isn't solely a conscious choice but the result of various conditions coalescing at that juncture. Consequently, the "perfect moment" to begin is not an arbitrary choice but when deterministic factors align to propel action.

Some critique this deterministic stance, emphasizing personal agency's role in molding our paths, viewing it as a potential surrender of personal accountability, though I refute that claim wholeheartedly. Yet, within this causality framework, such reactions too are outcomes of established determinants.

Grasping the equilibrium between determinism and agency is pivotal. It's not an acceptance of fate or a declaration of boundless free will, but a recognition of our place within a deterministic construct. This understanding calls for humility when faced with life's complexities and courage in exercising our influence.

Building upon our understanding of causality, determinism, and human agency, we can navigate to the intriguing intricacies of human desire and ambition. Often, we hear phrases like "I wish I was doing that," or "I wish I was that person." The typical response, "you can achieve that as well," may somewhat miss the essence of these expressions. What underpins these yearnings is not merely the possibility of achieving a specific outcome but rather a longing for an instantaneous transformation. The individual may indeed possess the capacity to undertake the journey toward that envisioned goal. Still, the pathway might appear daunting or

ambiguous, leading to a longing for a dramatic, external catalyst that would propel them into their desired circumstances. This yearning, it can be argued, is often fueled more by the anticipation of validation than by the actual experience, as I related from personal experience earlier in the book. As a result, human ambition frequently entwines with a complex matrix of validation-seeking, a craving for immediate gratification, and a reluctance or incapacity to navigate the path to the desired outcome. Recognizing these layers can pave the way for more empathetic, nuanced discussions about ambition, success, and the complexities of the human condition. And perhaps, through the process of reading this book, you will have stumbled across the exact sequence of words required to produce a psychochemical reaction in the brain that induces a state of peace and serenity. An opiate for the limbic system, quelling some of the existential dread or confusion that prevents one from living in the flow state with their deterministic existence. After all, witches and wizards cast spells through incantations–specific utterances meant to invoke supernatural forces, alluding to a very literal commanding power through language. So, if this is your causally dictated moment to come upon the "answer" you've been seeking, then congratulations.

CHAPTER THIRTY-NINE

The Illusion of Control and the Power of Probability

Let's reframe our understanding of the instinctual desire for control and consider how we can more effectively navigate the complexities of our social, professional, and personal lives by shifting our focus towards predictability and probability. This perspective shift serves not only to provide us with a more realistic framework for decision-making, but also to alleviate the undue stress and anxiety often associated with an illusory pursuit of control.

The crux of the argument is that control is not the end goal, but rather predictability. The human desire to control situations and environments is fundamentally rooted in a primal need for safety and predictability. We yearn for a consistent arrangement of factors and circumstances that can be easily processed and planned around, thereby satisfying our survival instinct. However, the concept of control is an illusion, especially when it comes to the actions and decisions of others. What we are really aiming for is a way to better play

the odds, much like a gambler at a roulette table. In the grand casino of life, we cannot control the spin of the wheel or the roll of the dice, but we can make strategic decisions that improve our chances of success, like betting on red or black, as opposed to the individual numbers in roulette. We are constantly making these "bets" in our day-to-day lives, optimizing for the best probable outcomes based on the available information and our understanding of the environment.

Drawing a parallel to the game of poker, we have no direct control over the hands dealt to other players or their subsequent actions. Yet, by observing behavior patterns and strategically interacting with the game environment, we can optimize our play. In other words, the focus is not on controlling others, but on increasing the probability of favorable outcomes through anticipatory actions and responses. However, we must be aware of the pitfalls of cognitive biases in our pursuit of predictability. Our perception of luck and probability can be distorted by these biases, causing us to see patterns where none exist, or to overlook them where they do. As we navigate the game of life, constantly reassessing our strategies is crucial to adapt to changing variables, and challenge our own assumptions.

When we shift our focus from control to predictability, we can reduce anxiety, improve decision-making, and increase our chances of success in all areas of life. It is about finding our power not in control but in the nuanced understanding of chance. This shift can lead to a healthier, more realistic, and ultimately more successful engagement with the world around us.

CHAPTER FORTY

Statistical Manipulation: Perverting the Odds

Our global human population hovers around the 8 billion mark, with approximately 150,000 of us departing this mortal coil each day. This constitutes a minuscule .00001% of the total populace. In other words, there's an overwhelming likelihood that you'll find yourself among the 99.99999% that prevails through any given day.

Such odds may not necessarily embolden individuals to adopt a more audacious approach to life or to shed their risk-averse tendencies. However, it should, at the very least, help to alleviate widespread anxieties regarding the perceived omnipresence of danger in our world. The odds of survival, regardless of one's situation, tip heavily in our favor. While certain professions might expose individuals to unconventional hazards—think oil rig operators or frontline soldiers—the prospect of surviving another day remains virtually intact. With mindful awareness of one's environment and a generous

serving of common sense, navigating life's uncertainties becomes a less daunting prospect.

So, as we traverse our individual paths, let's not allow fear to eclipse our perception of the world. Instead, let's remember that each new dawn presents a fresh opportunity for survival, growth, and exploration within the realm of life's vast potential.

Though we do have one particular real-world perpetrator of the statistician fear tactic, and it's one most Americans might remember from childhood.

The "Every 15 Minutes" program was launched in Canada during the mid 1990s, and was soon adopted by American law enforcement departments and agencies, such as California Highway Patrol. Though noble in its intentions, it presents an interesting case in examining the use and interpretation of statistics in influencing societal behavior. The program hinges on the terrifying fact that someone dies every 15 minutes due to drunk driving in the United States, aiming to deter teenagers from participating in this dangerous behavior.

However, if we flip the perspective, as suggested, the picture it presents may inadvertently convey a different message. Between these fatal accidents occurring every 15 minutes, there potentially exists a multitude of drunk-driving incidents that pass without fatal consequences. Consequently, an observant individual might infer that the chances of surviving a drunk driving incident are significantly higher than dying in one. It illustrates the oddity of statistical interpretations—the framing can drastically alter the narrative.

This is not to say that any form of drunk driving is acceptable or that it doesn't carry considerable risks, but it is to question the effectiveness of fear tactics that manipulate statistics for shock value. In some cases, such presentations can have unintended consequences by fostering a sense of invulnerability in young individuals, who are statistically more prone to take risks. In fact, various studies, such as the one by J. Arnett (1992), "Reckless behavior in adolescence: A developmental perspective," point out that adolescents have a propensity to seek stimulation while underestimating their innate vulnerabilities, which may contribute to risk-taking behaviors, including drunk driving. Either way, the data clearly indicates that scare tactics and dramatizations are ineffective at influencing permanent change to behavior.

A more balanced approach might involve a candid conversation about the realities and consequences of drunk driving, with an emphasis on personal responsibility, empathy towards potential victims, and the tangible, non-fatal consequences of drunk driving, such as legal troubles, hefty fines, and long-term damage to one's health and life opportunities. This comprehensive understanding of statistical information with a more nuanced presentation, free from fear tactics and manipulation, may yield more enduring behavioral changes. After all, meaningful conversations rooted in truth, respect, and authenticity can often have more lasting impacts than shock and awe statistics, especially considering the fact that teenagers have a subconscious need to resist authoritarian fiat dictates.

This reality of probabilistic confidence is intended to help promote intellectual assuredness for instinctive inclinations. The notion of "fortune favors the bold" suggests that audacity, often characterized by decisive risk-taking, can lead to rewards. Delving into this idea from biological and sociological perspectives can offer insights into the intrinsic value humans place on being "correct" and the influence of confidence.

From a biological standpoint, when individuals believe they are correct or receive affirmation of such a belief, the brain's reward system gets activated, primarily through the release of dopamine, a neurotransmitter associated with pleasure and reward. Evolutionarily, this mechanism makes sense. Our ancestors who made correct decisions in contexts like hunting or avoiding predators had better survival outcomes, and the pleasure associated with being right would have reinforced such behaviors.

Sociologically, correctness plays a pivotal role in social interactions and hierarchies. In historical contexts, those perceived as knowledgeable often held leadership positions, thereby influencing societal directions and decisions. Furthermore, correctness often signals alignment with group norms, enhancing an individual's position within the group and fostering unity.

Confidence, interestingly, can be as influential as actual correctness. Several reasons underpin this phenomenon:

1. Throughout history, confident individuals have been perceived as leaders, especially in challenging situations. Their decisiveness, even in the absence of objective correctness, could

rally group members, leading to collective actions that might not have occurred otherwise.

2. Humans have evolved to use heuristics, or mental shortcuts, for decision-making. A common heuristic involves deferring to those who seem confident or authoritative, assuming their confidence equates with correctness.

3. Cognitive dissonance theory posits that, when faced with conflicting ideas, people often shift their beliefs to align with those exuding confidence to avoid the discomfort of contradiction.

4. Confidence has a contagious quality. Observing confidence in others can bolster an individual's own assurance and beliefs.

5. In uncertain scenarios, a confident person reduces the perceived risk associated with decision-making. People often opt to follow a confident leader, as indecision might be seen as a greater risk.

While accuracy and facts are undeniably valuable, confidence occupies a significant space in influencing human actions and decisions. Consider charismatic leaders, be they cult figures or influential religious heads—their confidence draws multitudes, even though there is rarely any hard, empirical evidence to justify their conviction. If one lacks self-assuredness or a clear direction, it becomes tempting to embrace someone else's vision as a guiding star, perhaps becoming successful by association. Given our biological instincts and societal norms, it's evident that both truth and confidence will persistently mold our behaviors and societal interactions. There is one other important dimension of the conscious experience that

shapes our reality, one that finds us inclined to abandon ourselves to amazement.

CHAPTER FORTY-ONE

Perplexing Multiplex Complex

The propensity for perplexity: an element of the human condition that predisposes an individual or group of people towards a state of disbelief or bewilderment; correlating to the inability to comprehend complex systems or processes beyond the scope of their immediate understanding, and the inclination to chalk it up to supernatural influence or causation (e.g., gods, magic, etc.)

Throughout history, this perplexity often gave rise to supernatural explanations for phenomena that couldn't be otherwise understood. From attributing thunderstorms to the anger of gods, to invoking magic to explain the inexplicable, supernatural reasoning provided a way to make sense of the world and our place in it. These narratives served a dual purpose: they helped assuage our collective anxiety in the face of uncertainty, and they fostered a sense of connection and shared understanding within communities. The primal impulse to rally together against threats, both real and imagined, takes root in our animal survival reflex. Which is why the imagined or contrived threats will never be dispelled because our

perception will never allow for the scope of grace required to tolerate a limitless amount of uncertainty and unknown that evokes the fight-or-flight response.

As we turn our gaze to the future, it's crucial to challenge our preconceived notions of societal collapse. The apocalyptic scenes often portrayed in cinema, depicting a sudden and dramatic end to our way of life, may not be our destiny. The degradation of society may, in fact, be a far subtler, quieter process, akin to the hollow men in T.S. Eliot's masterful poem. This paraphrased quote from Milton Mayer describes the situation effectively.

> You wait for one great shocking occasion, thinking that others, when such a shock comes, will join with you in resisting somehow. But the one great shocking occasion, when tens or hundreds of thousands will join with you, never comes. If the last and worst act of the whole regime had come immediately after the first and smallest, thousands, yes, millions would have been sufficiently shocked. But of course, this isn't the way it happens. In between comes all the hundreds of little steps, some of them imperceptible, each of them preparing you not to be shocked by the next. ... And one day, too late, your principles, if you were ever sensible of them, all rush in upon you, and you see that everything—everything—has changed. Now you live in a world of hate and fear, and the people who hate and

fear do not even know it themselves; when everyone is transformed, no one is transformed.

~Milton Mayer

We may begin to observe an insidious change in our day-
to-day life. The price of commodities might incrementally
inch upwards, while our living spaces and incomes shrink.
Working hours could extend, casting a shadow over the time
we have for our loved ones, subtly shifting our emotional connections. As the world we once knew subtly fades away, we
might find ourselves continually adjusting our expectations,
trading dreams for survival. The societal fabric may warp and
strain under this new reality. Job security could evaporate like
a mirage, leaving only uncertainty. Fewer people might choose
to tie the knot, and children could become a rarity. As the
tangible world grows increasingly harsh, people might find
solace in the digital realm, obscuring their perception of their
lived reality. The aspirations we once harbored for our lives
might recede into the mist of memory, replaced by the harsh
reality of debt and poverty. Yet, amidst this, we may find ourselves being reassured by a hollow message of unity, prosper-
ity, and safety. The real collapse, then, might not be a sudden
cataclysm, but the gradual devolution of our society into a
state of learned helplessness and diminished self-worth. Thus,
the true challenge of our times may not lie in navigating a sudden disaster, but in recognizing and combating this quiet descent into a new form of serfdom.

I'd like to think there's a way out of the challenges we're
facing, and I believe the solutions suggested here offer a viable
means for at least coping with the incipient reality. While

community organization and efforts to maintain personal freedom are important, especially in the face of rising authoritarianism, it's likely that many people have grown complacent due to modern comforts and the numbing effects of constant media exposure. If any among you have the temerity to lead a movement, now is your chance.

CHAPTER FORTY-TWO

Dual Existence: Embracing a Dichotomous Perspective

The world, in its infinite variety and constant flux, presents a continuous dance of dichotomies: day and night, summer and winter. As one hemisphere basks in the midday sun, another slumbers under a blanket of stars. Similarly, while one part of the world shivers in winter's chill, another celebrates the life-giving warmth of summer.

This dual state of existence mirrors the constant ebb and flow of opportunities in our lives. It is a testament to the fact that our local circumstances, however immutable they might seem, are but a single thread in the vast tapestry of global existence. Recognizing this can help us transcend the limitations of our immediate environment, encouraging us to seek opportunities beyond our local horizons. If globalism is to be the prevailing ideology, may as well make use of it.

By viewing our lives in this broader, global context, we can optimize our ability to seize opportunities and cultivate

growth. This philosophy extends the wisdom of the old adage "make hay while the sun shines," urging us to not merely respond to local conditions, but actively seek "sunshine" wherever it may be.

Indeed, in an increasingly interconnected world, our "ecosystem placement" need not limit us. We can draw on global resources and networks to cultivate growth and opportunity in all seasons of our lives. By taking this expansive view, we allow ourselves to tap into a wider array of experiences and possibilities, thus enriching our personal and professional lives in a way that honors the dual state of existence that defines our world.

CHAPTER FORTY-THREE

A Hegelian Perspective

It's essential to recognize from the onset that Georg Wilhelm Friedrich Hegel's philosophy is both intricate and profound. The perspective offered here, drawing parallels between his dialectical method and the dichotomy of process vs. outcome thinking, is merely one interpretation of his comprehensive work. Bearing this in mind, we explore how Hegel's method sheds light on the nuances between a process-oriented and an outcome-oriented mindset, emphasizing its significance in understanding change and progress.

A process-oriented mind, according to Hegel's philosophy, aligns with the "thesis" stage of his dialectical method. In this stage, a situation or state of affairs exists in its own right, without yet being opposed or challenged. This is a mind focused on the present, on action and the doing, without any preoccupation with a future outcome. It is akin to the "becoming" in Hegel's view, where existence is not static but rather in a constant state of flux and evolution. Women and insecure men tend to have a hard time existing in a state of static

isolation, which aligns with the Hegelian notion of the process mind.

The outcome-oriented mind aligns with the "antithesis" stage in Hegel's dialectic. This mindset opposes the initial "thesis," as it is focused not on the existing state of affairs but on a future outcome or goal. This mind is concerned with "what could be," always looking forward and planning the path towards its objective. Typical of the industrious or pro-active father archetype.

But the crux of Hegel's philosophy lies in the "synthesis" stage, where the thesis and antithesis are resolved into a higher state of understanding or being. This could be interpreted as the ideal mindset that combines elements of both process and outcome-oriented thinking. This synthesis embodies the acknowledgement and understanding of the present moment (the process), while also keeping an eye on the desired outcome (the goal). The union of a man and woman, beyond the scope of simple reproductive biology, makes sense from this lens in particular.

From a Hegelian perspective, neither mindset—process-oriented nor outcome-oriented—is superior in isolation. Instead, they each play a vital role in our development and self-improvement, feeding into a larger dialectical process. The synthesis of these approaches allows us to engage fully in the present moment and the task at hand, while also maintaining an awareness of our broader goals and objectives. This dialectical mindset provides a holistic approach to growth, acknowledging the importance of both the journey and the destination in our personal and professional development.

In furthering our understanding of gender differences, another key area to examine is the varying degrees of spatial awareness between men and women. A body of research, including studies such as those conducted by Voyer, Voyer, and Bryden (1995), suggests that men tend to perform better on spatial tasks, such as mental rotation tasks and spatial navigation, whereas women tend to excel in object location memory and multitasking.

It is intriguing to consider these findings in the context of process-oriented versus outcome-oriented thinking. Traditionally, men's roles required them to navigate their surroundings for hunting and exploration (requiring strong spatial skills and outcome-focused planning). Meanwhile, women were often caregivers and gatherers, roles that necessitated an awareness of the immediate environment, object placement, and managing concurrent tasks (demonstrating a more process-oriented approach).

Theoretically, this could suggest a connection between the gender-based variations in spatial awareness and the tendency towards process or outcome-focused cognition. Men's historical tasks emphasized the end goal (the outcome—a successful hunt or exploration), perhaps fostering better spatial skills. In contrast, women's historical roles centered on managing the immediate environment and process (the gathering and caring tasks at hand), possibly enhancing their object location memory and multitasking skills.

While these differences may have evolutionary roots, we must remember that today's society is far removed from our hunter-gatherer ancestors. Our environments, education,

experiences, and societal norms influence our cognitive abilities and orientations significantly. Plus, it's worth noting that not all men and women fit into these general patterns, though acknowledging these gender variances is valuable for understanding our shared humanity and complexity. Recognizing these cognitive differences can enrich our appreciation of the diverse ways in which we perceive and interact with our world, whether through a process-oriented or outcome-oriented lens, or, ideally, through the synthesis of both.

The common ground between the gender divide and political divide could indeed revolve around fundamental misunderstandings or misconceptions about process versus outcome orientations. These issues could breed mistrust and inhibit cooperation, which may be further compounded by the motivation to conform or to meet perceived expectations.

In gender dynamics, traditional stereotypes often cast men as outcome-focused and women as process-oriented. Men are often expected to be decisive and results-driven, while women are perceived as more empathetic and relationship-focused. Such stereotypes could lead to miscommunications and misunderstandings, with each side misunderstanding or undervaluing the other's approach.

Similarly, in the political sphere, conservatives tend to focus on outcomes—law and order, economic growth, protection of traditional values—while liberals are often more concerned with the process, emphasizing the notions of inclusivity, fairness, and the pursuit of social justice. This fundamental difference in focus can lead to conflicting viewpoints and an inability to find common ground.

The motivation to lie, or to misrepresent one's beliefs or intentions, can come from a desire to fit into these prescribed roles or ideologies. For instance, an individual might suppress or distort their true views in order to align with their perceived gender role or political identity, contributing to further polarization.

By recognizing these process vs. outcome orientations and the potential distortions they can cause in our self-presentation, we might find a new perspective for understanding and potentially bridging these divides. This involves respecting the value of both process and outcome, and appreciating the diverse ways in which individuals and groups contribute to societal progression.

PART NINE

Future Outlooks and Transitions

The Inadvertent Exodus: When Artificial Intelligence Usurps Human Skills

In the dynamic age of digitization and automation, the progressive trend toward integrating Artificial Intelligence (AI) into everyday life seems inevitable. While this transition holds the promise of unprecedented efficiency and productivity, it also raises an essential question: What happens when the tools we create to assist us ultimately replace us?

Consider the average office environment. Tasks that once took hours, like data entry and analysis, can now be accomplished in mere minutes with AI. Software algorithms can sort and analyze large data sets more accurately and efficiently than their human counterparts. In customer service, AI-driven chatbots now handle routine inquiries, allowing representatives to focus on more complex tasks. Real-world examples of AI revolutionizing workflow are plenty, but there's a price to be paid.

The convenience offered by AI can create a double-edged sword. On one hand, we're freed from mundane, repetitive tasks, able to focus on more creative, strategic initiatives. Although we are already outsourcing our creativity to tools like Kaiber and MidJourney because, in the context of a soulless work environment, or even in the case of the ineffectual professional, the most creative responsibility is still ultimately a task of tedium. However, in outsourcing these tasks, we run the risk of falling out of practice, of losing the very skills that we've honed over a lifetime. The adage "use it or lose it" comes to mind.

The trend is not dissimilar to the advent of calculators. Once these devices became widely available, mental arithmetic began to fall by the wayside. Now, most people would reach for their smartphone to calculate a tip or work out a percentage rather than crunch the numbers in their head. It's not that they can't do the math; it's just easier and faster to let a device handle it.

The issue becomes more concerning when we extrapolate this trend to its logical conclusion. If we continue to offload tasks to AI, eventually, we might find ourselves in a world where human skills have been so eroded by disuse that we're no longer capable of performing tasks that were once second nature. In essence, by attempting to make our lives easier, we may be setting ourselves up for redundancy, supplanted by the very technology we created.

The concern here isn't necessarily about AI's ability to perform tasks more efficiently than humans but about what it means for our development and identity when we let go of the

tasks that helped us grow and define ourselves. Are we prepared to navigate a future where human skills become obsolete? A future where we're the bystanders in our own lives, mere supervisors of AI's labor? Though realistically, if we're being honest with ourselves, we know that supervision task will inevitably be outsourced to AI as well.

While this picture may seem dystopian, it's crucial to remember that we control the direction of AI development. AI serves us, not the other way around (for now.)

As we usher in this era of unprecedented technological growth, we need to ensure that we're not only creating efficient tools but also safeguarding our skills and our humanity. To navigate this uncertain future, we must balance the allure of convenience with the preservation of our unique human capabilities, crafting a world where AI and humans coexist and complement each other.

However, the advent of advanced artificial intelligence technologies has already significantly altered our perception of reality, having been initially wielded by intelligence agencies under the guise of "national security." (https://sgp.fas.org/crs/natsec/R45178.pdf) The public release of this technology is a curious development, one that aligns with events such as the 2016-2020 election cycles and coincides with an insidious societal shift. Societal problems often pave the way for state-endorsed solutions, and in this context, the rise of AI could serve to create a scapegoat for a crusade against misinformation.

By equipping the public with AI capabilities, a landscape is crafted where anyone might be a potential antagonist, which

in turn could warrant unprecedented security measures. This harks back to the fundamental issue of identity and the overwhelming uncertainty brought about by AI's capacity to create highly realistic facsimiles of people. An overflow of AI entities could shroud the internet in a veil of illusion, and eventually, real human interactions might become indistinguishable from AI interfaces. A quick Google search reveals that almost half of all Internet traffic in 2023 can be attributed to bots, and with the various tools that allow users to algorithmically generate content, it's conceivable that a decent amount of online engagement is already happening without any direct human involvement whatsoever.

This state of confusion could prompt the implementation of a mandated digital identity verification system, claimed to be the only way to ensure the authenticity of human interactions online. This would herald an era of total information control, thereby tipping the scales of the internet's dual nature—its potential for anonymity—which has been both a boon and a bane for the free exchange of information.

The proposed digital identity platform would essentially mark the end of online anonymity, enabling the state to trace any form of misinformation back to its source, and administer punitive measures. Societal compliance is seemingly inevitable, as seen from current trends, despite the blatant infringement on privacy rights. Sam Altman's WorldCoin seems to be paving the way for this future, and users are already signing up to get their retinas scanned.

Institutions from the corporate and financial sectors would likely support this protocol, given the high stakes

involved in their transactions. For instance, banks would not risk conducting business with a potential AI entity. This digital identity would be ubiquitously used for any data or financial transaction, reinforcing the state's grip on information flow.

Those opposing this paradigm would likely be branded as political dissidents or "misinformation terrorists," echoing past societal responses to individuals who challenge prevailing systems. The treatment of these individuals will serve as a chilling testament to the profound implications of this AI-induced societal shift.

The control and direction of generative AI technologies, led by the likes of Microsoft and Google, are on a path towards challenging the very notion of independent thought. An initial focus on curbing usages that violate prevailing societal norms, as seen in the biases of AI like ChatGPT, soon opens the door for wider censorship. Any information conflicting with the established narrative can potentially be suppressed under the guise of bias, ethics, or even copyright laws. Intellectual property rights, a potent motivator for many, are likely to encourage adherence to impending security measures.

These actions will significantly hinder critical thinking and objectivity, as all potentially threatening information could simply be labeled as AI-generated deviations from the accepted "truth" or as infringements on perceived "rights." The dependence on claims of foreign interference, like during the 2016-2020 elections, would no longer be necessary. The surge in AI-generated content has already accustomed the public to this technology and its nuances. Consequently, people may question the validity of all information, yet remain powerless

to discern empirical reality without safeguards in place to authenticate one's experience (Lazer et al., 2018).

In this climate of uncertainty, the proposed digital ID system may be welcomed as a solution to the very problem instigated by the establishment. The manipulation of reality perception would thus be securely in the hands of those in power. In our technology-saturated world, eluding such a system and maintaining free will may become virtually unattainable.

Despite the current perception of AI technology as a benign or even beneficial tool, it will soon be embedded in every aspect of digital life. All content generated with AI assistance will be tied to the digital ID, allowing for retrospective scrutiny should it be deemed "problematic." Unless society collapses completely, this inevitable evolution appears unstoppable.

As we edge closer to the creation of artificial general intelligence (AGI) through technological advancements, we're prompted to delve deeper into the concept of free will that we touched upon earlier. Where does the scope of free will find its boundary and do the same circumstances apply to artificial intelligence? The locus of free will, in which constituent part of the individual, does it truly reside? Our current understanding of the mind, as far as we comprehend, is deeply embedded in the intricate workings of the brain. Consequently, we perceive this mind as the self, linking it intrinsically to our notions of personality and character. However, if this mental realm originates from the brain, a complex ensemble of individual cells, why does our extension of the free will framework halt at this cellular level?

This query invites us to delve further. Should we not extrapolate this concept of free will to the microscopic organelles within these cells, the molecules composing these organelles, the atoms forming these molecules, and even the subatomic particles that build these atoms? If each subsequent layer of complexity is a construction upon its predecessor, it intimates that our conception of free will is merely an emergent phenomenon of fundamental mechanical processes, operating stealthily beneath our conscious grasp. The mind, it thus appears, is not a tangible entity; it is a remarkable reaction, a symphony of natural forces in motion. What we perceive as the aggregate self is a choreographed sequence of biological events, unfolding simultaneously and sequentially. Each identifiable trait is a manifestation of these multifarious interactions, materializing in a discernible form only when the time comes for this inherent characteristic to make its debut on the stage of the external environment.

A question naturally arises from this contemplation: what about cancer cells that emerge within the human body? Should we consider a form of free will that perhaps suffuses the universe, either subconsciously or unconsciously, by human standards? It could be posited that cancer cells express this faculty as they rebel against the collective command of the organism, choosing, as it were, to follow their own self-serving itinerary. In their pursuit of resource consumption, they wreak havoc within their environment, a course of action that invariably leads to their eventual self-destruction. Let us recall Henrietta Lacks, a cancer patient from the 1950s, whose DNA has remarkably outlived her, continuing to proliferate in the form of tumor cells. Here we find cells carrying human DNA,

essentially undying, surviving far beyond the conscious existence of the individual traditionally deemed the embodiment
of free will. Yet, it would be unusual to encounter someone
ready to confer personhood on such a cellular assembly, a
point underscored by pro-choice activism.

One might counter that this is not a display of free will,
but rather a deviation from the natural biological course of the
body. Yet, I would propose that a parallel assertion could be
drawn regarding the body itself, as an integral unit within the
broader societal structure it forms. When we reconfigure our
understanding of consciousness or the mind considering
panpsychism, the human mind ceases to be a singular, extraordinary entity. It becomes, instead, a metaphorical veneer we
utilize to denote the sub-categorized set of intricate biochemical interactions that constitute the inner life of an organism
within a community.

As we stand on the precipice of this digital singularity,
where the lines between machine and man, reality and illusion,
and autonomy and programming blur, we are compelled to
revisit and redefine our understanding of identity, agency, and
humanity itself. The melding of AI into our lives is not merely
a technological revolution, but a profound transformation of
our societal fabric, challenging the very essence of what it
means to be human. While we marvel at the advancements AI
promises and grapple with the existential questions it raises, it
is imperative that we proceed with intention, foresight, and an
unwavering commitment to preserving the human spirit and
resist the allure of the path of least resistance. Only through
conscious reflection and proactive decision-making can we

hope to shape a future where technology amplifies our humanity, rather than diminishing it.

CHAPTER FORTY-FIVE

Impermanence and Loss

The concept of loss is profound and central to our human experience. However, its significance tends to be heightened at the point of immediate contrast between what was and what now is. This stark juxtaposition creates a sense of void and engenders a feeling of loss. As time passes and a new paradigm takes shape, this sense of loss can diminish and become less relevant as we adjust to the new reality. This subject may be especially relevant to the human species at large, as we accelerate down an increasingly precarious path towards an uncertain future.

This notion resonates with the psychological concept known as "hedonic adaptation" or "the hedonic treadmill." This theory suggests that people tend to return to a relatively stable level of happiness despite major positive or negative events or life changes. A study published in the *Journal of Personality and Social Psychology* titled "Lottery Winners and Accident Victims: Is Happiness Relative?" explores this concept. In the study, both lottery winners and accident victims, over time, showed a similar level of happiness to individuals who

had not experienced such drastic life events. The constant flux and impermanence of life can indeed make it challenging for individuals, particularly adults, to find a solid grounding. As we grow older and gain more life experiences, we become more aware of the transient nature of life, which can lead to feelings of insecurity or uncertainty. This is evident in the mid-life crisis phenomenon, a period of emotional turmoil in middle adulthood characterized by a desire to make significant life changes, as outlined by psychologist Elliott Jaques in his seminal 1965 paper.

Learning to navigate this ever-changing landscape is critical for our well-being and resilience. Embracing the concept of impermanence can help us to adapt more readily to changes and loss. The practice of mindfulness, which emphasizes living in the present moment, is one approach that has been shown to be effective in managing change and reducing anxiety about the future.

Psychologist Mihaly Csikszentmihalyi, in his book *Flow: The Psychology of Optimal Experience*, proposes that achieving a state of "flow," or complete immersion in an activity, can help individuals find fulfillment and happiness, despite the impermanence of life. While loss and impermanence are inevitable aspects of life, our ability to adjust to new paradigms and live in the present moment can help us navigate these challenges and lead more fulfilled and resilient lives.

CHAPTER FORTY-SIX

Ideologies: Emphasizing Outcome versus Emphasizing Experience

Peoples' ideological differences might hinge on whether they place emphasis on the outcome or the experience. This dichotomy plays a significant role in the distinct outlooks of conservative and liberal individuals.

Conservatives often lean towards an outcome-focused perspective, valuing the reliability and structure of established systems. By adhering to traditional frameworks, they seek to minimize uncertainty and ensure predictable outcomes. This also has the consequence of producing more concrete tenets of their fundamental ideology, represented by slogans such as "build the wall" or "lock her up." They are clear, direct, and literal. The security of a known destination or direction is prioritized over the potential novelty or excitement of the journey. Whether not the goal is attainable is a separate matter, but in terms of animal logic and the application of Occam's

Razor, it certainly adheres to what we have discussed in terms of natural path of least resistance.

On the other hand, liberals are more likely to value the journey, or the experience, over the destination. They emphasize the process and the progress, even if the outcome is unknown or uncertain. This experience-focused perspective is often linked to the virtues of progressivism and influences their rhetoric accordingly. The phrases "black lives matter" and "love is love" lack specific, impactful details, and can be tautologically banal or devoid of meaningful content. While they aim to inspire and unify, their vagueness may dilute their effectiveness in rallying individuals toward a cohesive vision of progress. The emphasis is not necessarily on knowing the exact destination or having a foolproof method to get there, but on feeling validated in the journey towards an abstract ideal of progress and improvement.

This divergence in emphasis between outcome and experience isn't necessarily a choice; rather, it seems to be an emergent property of one's intrinsic psychology and genetic makeup, shaped by environmental interaction. It's as if our heuristic models, or personal sensibilities, are naturally oriented on a spectrum between outcome and experience focus, each with its own strengths and challenges.

In understanding these divergent ideological lenses, we can better appreciate the strengths and limitations of each perspective and foster a more nuanced dialogue. Acknowledging this complex interplay between our psychology, genetics, and environment can open new pathways for cooperation, mutual understanding, and constructive societal evolution.

Another way to interpret the ideological divide is to consider the variation between those who directly initiate change, taking responsibility for and shaping their own outcomes, and those who motivate social structures to implement change on their behalf, hoping to benefit from the indirect outcomes.

A notable example of this variance can be seen in entrepreneurial endeavors, typically a domain where individuals take direct action to effect change. Entrepreneurs epitomize the philosophy of taking personal responsibility, venturing into uncharted territories, and creating value for themselves and society at large. The tech industry in Silicon Valley, for instance, is brimming with such individuals who shape their outcomes through innovation and persistence, irrespective of the risks.

On the other hand, there are those who advocate for changes in social structures with the hope of benefiting indirectly from the outcomes. For instance, some individuals advocate for social safety nets like universal healthcare or minimum income guarantees. They hope that these systemic changes would yield benefits for them and others, often citing issues like income inequality or healthcare disparity as evidence of systemic injustice. It's essential to remember that broad stroke generalizations can lead to oversimplification. It's not always a case of one group merely claiming victimhood, while the other lifts itself by its bootstraps. For instance, while it's true that the free-market system has uplifted billions from poverty over the past century, it's also evident that observable inequities persist in many societies, which need addressing for continued progress. Therefore, a balanced

perspective that acknowledges both personal responsibility and systemic improvements could lead to more constructive dialogues and solutions. Though it's essential to address economic disparities and societal discord, it's equally crucial to recognize when political ideologies evolve in dangerous ways. Let's briefly delve into the concerning phenomenon of certain political factions displaying characteristics akin to death cults.

Could one interpret the network of modern leftists as having attributes resembling a death cult? An objective observer might see a similarity between elective abortion and ancient pagan practices of sacrifice for a bountiful harvest or, perhaps, just a future free from the financial demands of children. Medical procedures like gender reassignment surgeries can be viewed as a physical, lifelong commitments to an ideology. Continuous medication prescriptions post-procedure could be seen as sort of daily prayer ritual, or more accurately a communion ritual, analogous to ingesting the body of Christ through the process of transubstantiation. Moreover, the idea of encouraging dissent against differing views, including those of one's own family, hints at efforts to align individuals more closely with a singular belief system. And the emphasis on personal experience and hedonistic impulse can be seen as challenging the established notion of objective, formalized reality. Yes, I suppose one could interpret that. But it's still important to refrain from making broad stroke generalizations about any one particular group of people based on singular dimensions of identity, even when it comes to professed political sensibilities.

The Fulfillment Triad

There exists an interesting interplay between personal aptitude, accessible opportunities, and one's interests. This triad shapes the trajectory of our life's work, achievements, and, importantly, the sense of fulfillment derived from our pursuits. The subject of discovering purpose in an existential void revolves around this very model, which, although not perfect, provides a semblance of a roadmap as we journey towards our common and inevitable end.

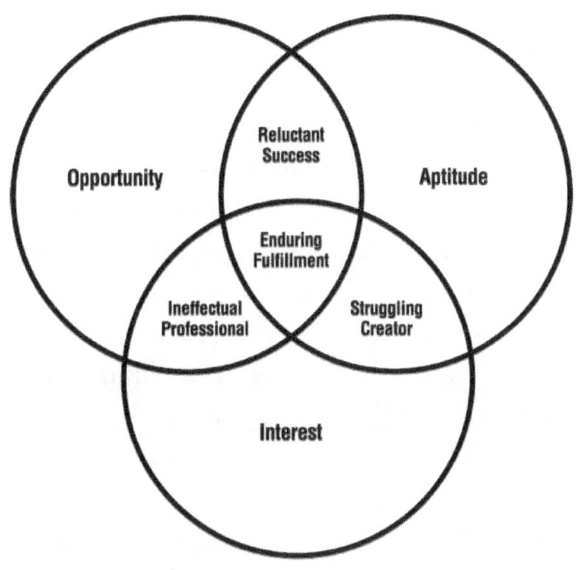

The Struggling Creator is characterized by an individual possessing both aptitude and interest, yet lacking opportunity. They may be highly skilled and passionate but lack the resources, networks, or circumstances necessary to fully express or apply their abilities. This could be the gifted artist in a rural area with limited access to artistic outlets, or the brilliant coder born in a low-income neighborhood without sufficient technological resources. Research, like that conducted by the Equality of Opportunity Project (Chetty, et al., 2014), indicates that socioeconomic status and geography can significantly impact access to opportunities, contributing to a gap between potential and realization. The Struggling Creator often grapples with feelings of frustration or dissatisfaction as they yearn to fully express their capabilities and follow their passions.

Within this context, the notion of "opportunity" must be broadened beyond the conventional understanding of job vacancies or specific roles to be fulfilled. It can represent a nurturing social environment or community that validates and appreciates our efforts. Consider the example of a band member who doesn't initially see themselves as a competent musician. However, sustained encouragement from their peers and audience—if met with even a lukewarm interest in music—can cultivate an inner sense of motivation to persist along the path. Even if a successful career in music doesn't manifest, the validation and appreciation from one's community can provide a gratifying experience. A supportive ecosystem that reinforces the message "we want you here" contributes significantly towards a fulfilling or at least a stable life. This, of course, is predicated on the assumption that such an

ecosystem is neither toxic nor harmful in some direct or indirect fashion (i.e., the industry culture of decadence and hedonism.) However, our journey, even when met with support from our community, often necessitates a confrontation with the "shadow" notion discussed earlier. This encounter poses its own set of trials and assumptions and doesn't necessarily guarantee the attainment of the authentic outcome we envisage. The path of self-discovery is seldom linear or predictable, and therein lies its complexity.

The Ineffectual Professional is an individual caught between good fortune and interest, but devoid of aptitude. This person has access to opportunities and exudes a sense of passion toward their pursuits, yet lacks the natural talent or skill set necessary for success. This could be the enthusiastic but less talented musician in a successful band, or the passionate academic who struggles with complex research methodologies. Studies, such as the work of Ericsson, et al. (1993) on deliberate practice, indicate that, while consistent practice and effort enhance skills, one's innate disposition is crucial for elevated expertise in a particular discipline, especially as it helps individuals commit to rigorous training effectively. Thus, the Ineffectual Professional may experience feelings of inadequacy and impostor syndrome, constantly trying to compensate for their perceived lack of ability or commitment. But the path to mastery varies for everyone, as evident in prodigies who showcase exceptional skill at a young age. For instance, Wolfgang Amadeus Mozart composed his first music pieces between ages 4 and 5 and performed for European royalty by age 6 (Melograni, P. 2007), negating Malcolm Gladwell's "10,000 hour rule" theory. A quick search on YouTube

reveals child prodigies displaying advanced musical talents, from 6-year-olds playing at Carnegie Hall standards to 2-year-olds keeping rhythm on a drum kit, seemingly by instinct. This suggests that certain innate qualities determine our potential for mastery, regardless of the amount of practice.

The Reluctant Success resides in the overlap of aptitude and opportunity but lacks interest. They have the skills and the chance to apply them yet lack the passion that often drives ambition and personal fulfillment. This might be the high-performing business executive who yearns for a career in painting, or the talented athlete pressured into sports by their family but longing for a different path. While a lack of intrinsic motivation can lead to reduced job satisfaction and creativity, certain types of extrinsic motivation can synergistically combine with low levels of intrinsic motivation, resulting in heightened employee satisfaction and performance. Despite such potential synergies, the Reluctant Success may still feel trapped or unfulfilled, achieving external measures of success while internally feeling discontented or disconnected from their work.

To navigate this triad and ultimately attain a state of fulfillment and success, a person must engage in transformative modalities: skills enhancement, opportunity creation, and passion cultivation.

Skill Enhancement can pave the way for a Struggling Creator's transformation into success. This doesn't just mean honing existing talents; it's also about acquiring new skills to open more doors. Both formal education and informal learning – like online courses, mentorships, and apprenticeships – play a

role in this journey. A study by Hershbein and Kahn (2018) found that regions hit hardest by the Great Recession witnessed a rise in skill requirements for job postings, notably in routine-cognitive roles. This points to a shift towards routine-biased technologies, amplifying the demand for skilled workers, particularly in IT and trades. For those in the arts, it could mean learning a new instrument or delving into music theory. However, achieving mastery is a journey that demands patience and humility, understanding that there's always room for growth.

Opportunity Creation is essential for both the Struggling Creator and the Ineffectual Professional. This could involve networking, entrepreneurship, or advocating for societal and policy changes that enhance opportunity equity. As Granovetter's (1973) Strength of Weak Ties theory suggests, even distant social connections can open doors to unforeseen opportunities. For Ineffectual Professionals, creating opportunities may also mean seeking different roles or fields where their unique blend of interests and skills may be more valued.

Passion Cultivation is especially important for the Reluctant Success. The cultivation of passion is a dynamic process that entails exploring new domains, fostering curiosity, and aligning one's work with personal values. Research by Vallerand et al. (2003) found that passion can be developed through engagement and identification with an activity. The Reluctant Success might need to take calculated risks, possibly stepping away from established success, to pursue more fulfilling paths.

The fundamental premise here is that authentic transformation, particularly in becoming a "better" person, may not

be as straightforward or even attainable as we generally consider. Rather than undergoing a profound metamorphosis, individuals may primarily utilize their cognitive skills to develop nuanced variations of their existing behavioral patterns, which are deeply ingrained from past experiences.

The role of therapy, oftentimes seen as a self-improvement pathway, also comes under scrutiny in this light. Instead of purely being a tool for personal growth, therapy could be seen as a training platform for mastering the art of manipulation. Once familiarized with the standard psychological jargon and therapeutic expressions, an individual—especially someone conditioned or with a predisposition for manipulation—could weave these into their new behavioral matrix. This would enable them to influence others more effectively, particularly those who might interpret these therapeutic buzzwords as an indication that the person has engaged in serious self-improvement work.

Survivability, seen through the lens of adaptability, is inherently context dependent. In every realm of our being, we occupy a certain percentile that others may view with either disdain or envy, mirroring the vast spectrum of human diversity.

Consider the domain of physical fitness. If you possess the ability to run continuously for a period or engage in calisthenics, you find yourself in a favorable position relative to an estimated 18–40% of Americans. For this group, the prospect of undertaking these basic physical activities might range from extraordinarily challenging to downright impossible. This, in essence, illustrates our relative adaptive capacities. What one

might regard as mundane or effortless, another might deem an enviable feat. In a world of diverse ecosystems and circumstances, every adaptation, however seemingly inconsequential, carves out its niche of suitability. This variance provides an intriguing insight into our collective social stratification, and, more profoundly, the spectrum of human potential.

Continuing the analysis, it becomes clear that our life trajectories are largely shaped by a complex interplay of innate predispositions and environmental factors. Humans are not created in a vacuum. Our abilities, skills, and potential are inseparable from the conditions and circumstances in which they are nurtured and expressed.

Consider the hypothetical scenario of an individual with a natural talent for comedy writing. Without exposure to the art of humor, the encouragement to express it, or the tools to hone this craft, this inherent talent may never come to light. The potential is present, but the circumstances to unveil it are not. This creates a kind of hidden potential that often goes unnoticed, a loss not just for the individual, but for society at large.

Now take the example of legendary basketball player Michael Jordan. If born in an era before the sport's invention or in a culture where basketball was not accessible, his exceptional athletic abilities may never have been discovered. It's not that his potential would be any less; rather, the environmental circumstances to recognize and utilize this potential would be lacking.

Furthermore, the value society places on specific skills or attributes heavily influences our perceptions of success and

self-worth. If an individual's abilities or talents do not align with what society deems valuable or prestigious, they may feel marginalized or unsuccessful, even though they might possess great potential in their area of expertise. This analysis underscores the importance of striving to create access to environments that value and encourage the traits a community member might possess.

In essence, understanding this interplay of predispositions and environment can serve as a catalyst for self-discovery and self-acceptance, further enhancing our personal growth and fulfillment. This knowledge allows us to better navigate our life paths, armed with the realization that our worth isn't solely defined by societal standards but also by our inherent potential and the unique contributions we can make to our world.

Continuing from this perspective, we can infer that procrastination is not merely an attribute of laziness, as it is commonly misunderstood. Rather, it is a complex emotional response influenced by factors such as fear, lack of inspiration, and potential misalignment with our inherent interests or talents. Procrastination can be perceived as a psychological defense mechanism against undertaking tasks that are perceived as daunting, challenging, or not aligning with our immediate interests. It often emerges from a fear of failure or a lack of confidence. The fear of appearing incompetent or being judged negatively by others can deter us from initiating a task, leading us to delay it indefinitely.

A task that seems tedious or unfulfilling can also lead to procrastination, as the lack of immediate gratification or joy can diminish one's motivation. In this sense, procrastination

can serve as a subconscious guide, steering us away from activities or career paths that may not resonate with our intrinsic interests or talents. Though it is important to note that essential tasks can't always be avoided. When faced with an impending deadline or the urgent necessity of a task, we tend to overcome procrastination, driven by the stress-induced biochemical reactions that stimulate action. This adaptive response can become our routine way of handling tasks that we'd rather avoid. While it can potentially work if we have the necessary skills for the task, it can also lead to chronic stress and emotional exhaustion.

This understanding of procrastination suggests a need for introspection and self-compassion. Recognizing the underlying fears or lack of alignment can help us navigate our emotional landscape and potentially guide our decisions towards more fulfilling pursuits. This awareness can also prompt us to seek strategies to overcome fears and build confidence, mitigating the stress and emotional fatigue associated with chronic procrastination. Thus, understanding procrastination not as a sign of laziness but as an emotional response influenced by various internal and external factors is critical for both personal growth and productivity.

The Digital Paradigm

Our society's rapid and pervasive digitalization, coupled with the explosion of social media platforms, has given birth to the attention economy, an economic system where human attention is treated as a scarce commodity (Goldhaber, 1997).

The Basic Attention Token (BAT) and Brave web browser are perfect examples of this phenomenon. Developed by Brendan Eich, the creator of JavaScript and co-founder of Mozilla, BAT aims to revolutionize the way we approach online advertising by directly linking advertisers, publishers, and users, thus eliminating intermediaries and enhancing user privacy (Eich & Bondy, 2018).

From a historical and sociological perspective, the Basic Attention Token represents a significant shift in the way we perceive and value attention. The emergence of the BAT and similar models can be traced back to the birth of mass media, particularly the print and broadcast industries, where advertisers started to pay for the potential attention of consumers.

With the advent of digital media and the internet, the scale of this phenomenon expanded dramatically. Digital platforms, powered by advanced algorithms, could capture, measure, and monetize attention in ways that were impossible in the traditional media landscape (Goldhaber, 1997).

The BAT, introduced in 2017, was one of the first solutions to formalize this shift by assigning a specific monetary value to attention in a bid to address the inefficient and often intrusive nature of digital advertising (Eich & Bondy, 2018). By leveraging blockchain technology, BAT sought to create a transparent and equitable marketplace for attention, wherein users are rewarded for their engagement with content.

The commodification of attention reflects broader societal shifts toward intangible goods and services. In the digital age, value is increasingly derived from data, information, and human cognition. Attention, which underpins all these elements, has consequently become a precious resource. The BAT and similar models could thus be seen as a response to these transformations, seeking to capitalize on the increasingly valuable resource of human attention.

However, this shift also carries implications for societal norms and values. The commodification of attention might lead to heightened levels of distraction and decreased capacity for deep engagement, with societal emphasis on rapid, often superficial engagement with content. The BAT, while aiming to mitigate some of the invasive and disruptive elements of the digital advertising industry, still operates within an attention economy, thus reinforcing the notion that attention is a commodity to be bought and sold.

The emergence of interactive platforms like TikTok, where live streamers emulate video game non-player characters (NPCs), is another facet of this attention economy. The concept involves users purchasing virtual gifts as a means of triggering certain reactions, effectively transforming passive viewing into an interactive experience. The potency of such user engagement models in capturing attention has been highlighted in numerous studies and essays, with one indicating that interactive video elements can enhance user engagement substantially (Brame, C. J. 2016).

The electronic girlfriend experience, also known as e-girl experience, signifies another dimension of the attention economy where companionship, traditionally considered an intimate, offline experience, is commodified in the online space. Such experiences typically involve virtual interaction that simulates a romantic or platonic relationship, often involving elements of role-playing and emotional support. Research has suggested that the popularity of these experiences could be attributed to factors such as social isolation, ease of access, and the increasing normalization of virtual relationships (Turkle, 2011).

What does this tell us about our society? At its core, the attention economy reveals an evolving nuance between technology and human interaction. As we delve deeper into the digital age, human attention has not only become a valuable resource but also a currency that shapes the contours of our online experiences. Simultaneously, the commodification of traditionally offline experiences like companionship indicates a societal shift towards virtual spaces for social interaction.

And because this is the path of least resistance for many who seek social engagement, it's almost guaranteed to increase in popularity. In particular, the NPC trend and associated cultural phenomena also allude to a deeper, unrealized need to assert influence over a situation, or engage within a social sphere in order to produce an outcome, trivial though that outcome may be.

Nonetheless, it is important to consider the potential ramifications of such trends. The commodification of attention might lead to an increased prevalence of manipulative practices designed to hijack our attention, while the normalization of virtual relationships could impact our ability to engage in offline social interactions. As such, it becomes crucial to retain the human element in our daily lives and understand that the hard-won victories will always be the most rewarding.

Final Words

If you read through this book in one sitting, in its entirety, I commend you. Though it is not particularly lengthy, it is certainly dense, and probably not very fun, so I hope you gained something from the experience. And if not, at least you will know to avoid literature of this nature in the future. You'll be better informed and know what to look out for whenever a book suggestion comes your way. You'll say, "This is reminiscent of that one book by that one guy," and you will move right along. And hey, I don't blame you. But if that is the case, well then, you did gain something: a refined insight into the nature of self-published reading material. So, this whole escapade wasn't for naught.

However, if you found any of the subject matter in this book to be compelling, I encourage you to explore those ideas in greater detail. Though more importantly, I hope you are encouraged to seek out the paradoxical pillars of reality and define the observable boundary of axiomatic truth. Challenge any of your pre-conceived notions of the world, or your presence within it. Stress-test every belief you've ever held and see what you're left with. It's truly remarkable what you can achieve from life when you approach it with unbridled curiosity and an inclination to experiment. You might end up in a

Super Bowl commercial for a national beer brand or find yourself participating in a cross-country solar car race throughout the continent of Australia (both of which happened to me).

Drawing inspiration from a story often attributed to Cherokee origin (though its authenticity is questionable), there are said to be two wolves inside of us: one that does us no harm and another that leads to our downfall. Given this inner dichotomy, we can sometimes be our own worst enemy. However, considering the notion that the enemy of our enemy is our friend, and the sage advice to keep friends close and enemies closer, it raises the question: Which wolf is truly in our best interest to nourish? The analysis requires keen understanding of nuance. Were such aphorisms and parables intended to be linked together? Probably not, but if they are true in their own regard, yet confounded when applied in association with each other, it would indicate that truth is fundamentally contextual and within certain boundaries of situational perception. As we previously discussed, the notion that truth is only valid in isolation could impact our understanding of the objective reality surrounding us. Best be wise to it.

If you ever find yourself paralyzed by uncertainty, unsure of your next move, remember that the hesitation of saying "I don't know" is often our mind's way of rationalizing our fear of insufficient information. While no one holds the key to absolute certainty, many still choose to forge ahead. Embrace this mindset to push yourself into action, even when caution feels more natural. Seize small moments of uncertainty, like sampling a dish you've never tried before or starting a

conversation with a stranger, to bolster your resilience and adaptability.

Though, if the structures of society seem too complex or restrictive, remember that your path will unfold as it's meant to, whether you act or remain still. Don't be consciously held back by societal notions of failure; they don't define your unique reality, so ignore those who claim to know it all from their pedestals of privilege and trust your own instincts. When the system challenges you, confront it with unwavering courage and belief in yourself. Don't fear the loss of material possessions; often, true fulfillment is found in simplicity and austerity. After all, it led Siddhartha Gautama to profound enlightenment, and those who resonate with such a disposition might find truth in Samuel Johnson's words: "He who makes a beast of himself gets rid of the pain of being a man."

The system does not care about your individual existence outside of the value you provide to the collective, even if it's at the expense of your own well-being. So don't feel afraid to be the animal that nature intended. Cry "Havoc!" and let slip the dogs of war that exist within you. There is a reason why Richard "Sky King" Russell moved so many people with his bold act of defiance, and it's because he represented the wayward, disillusioned soul, yearning to be free from the abysmal mundanity of what we come to accept as reality. Even though it was a comparatively short joyride, and resulted in his own demise, it was likely one of the rare moments in his lifetime where he truly felt alive. The nexus of liberation and fulfillment that few of us will ever reach.

References

PART ONE: FOUNDATIONS OF CONSCIOUSNESS
AND PERSONAL DEVELOPMENT

CHAPTER ONE: CONTEXTUALIZING OUR
CONSCIOUSNESS

Krupnik, Igor. "Database analysis of the Inuit nomenclature." *Canadian Geographer* 55, no. 1 (2011).
https://doi.org/10.1111/j.1541-0064.2010.00345.x

Whorf, B.L. *Language, Thought, and Reality: Selected Writings.* Technology Press of Massachusetts Institute of Technology: Cambridge, Mass., 1956.

Kay, P., and Kempton, W. "What is the Sapir-Whorf hypothesis?" *American Anthropologist* 86, no. 1 (1984): 65–79.
https://doi.org/10.1525/aa.1984.86.1.02a00050

Boroditsky, L. "Does language shape thought? Mandarin and English speakers' conceptions of time." *Cognitive Psychology* 43, no. 1 (2001): 1–22.
https://doi.org/10.1006/cogp.2001.0748

CHAPTER TWO: THE INTERPLAY OF EMOTION
AND COGNITION IN CONSCIOUSNESS: A
NEUROSCIENCE PERSPECTIVE

Kandel, E.R., Schwartz, J.H., Jessell, T.M., Siegelbaum, S.A., Hudspeth, A.J., and Mack, S. *Principles of Neural Science*. McGraw-Hill Professional Publishing, 2012.

Carhart-Harris, R.L., Erritzoe, D., Williams, T., Stone, J.M., Reed, L.J., Colasanti, A., Tyacke, R.J., Leech, R., Malizia, A.L., Murphy, K., Hobden, P., Evans, J., Feilding, A., Wise, R.G., and Nutt, D.J. "Neural correlates of the psychedelic state as determined by fMRI studies with psilocybin." *Proc Natl Acad Sci USA*, 109, no. 6 (2012): 2138–43.

Damasio, A. R. *Descartes' Error: Emotion, Reason, and the Human Brain*. G.P. Putnam's Sons, 1994.

CHAPTER FOUR: ASTRAL AND EXISTENTIAL ORIGINS

Fowler, J. H., and Christakis, N. A. "Dynamic spread of happiness in a large social network: longitudinal analysis over 20 years in the Framingham Heart Study." *BMJ* (2008): 337.

Singhal, A. (2019). "The positive deviance approach to designing and implementing behavior change interventions." In *The Handbook of Persuasion and Social Marketing*.

Dweck, C. S. *Mindset: The New Psychology of Success*. Random House Digital, Inc., 2006.

PART TWO: EXPLORING SELF-IMPROVEMENT AND BIAS

CHAPTER SEVEN: CONFLUENCE OF COGNITIVE BIASES: SHAPING THE SOCIOCULTURAL LANDSCAPE

Ross, L., and Ward, A. "Naive Realism in Everyday Life: Implications for Social Conflict and Misunderstanding." In *Values and Knowledge*, edited by T. Brown, E. S. Reed, & E. Turiel, 103–135. Psychology Press, 1996.

Miller, D.T., and Ratner, R.K. "The disparity between the actual and assumed power of self-interest." *Journal of Personality and Social Psychology* 74, no. 1 (1998): 53–62.

Brehm, J.W. *A Theory of Psychological Reactance.* Academic Press, 1966.

CHAPTER NINE: THE PARADOX OF NARCISSISM: CONFIDENCE, COMPETENCE, AND INNATE ABILITIES

Paulhus, D.L. "Interpersonal and intrapsychic adaptiveness of trait self-enhancement: A mixed blessing?" *Journal of Personality and Social Psychology* 74, no. 5 (1998): 1197–1208. https://doi.org/10.1037/0022-3514.74.5.1197

Twenge, J.M., and Campbell, W.K. *The Narcissism Epidemic: Living in the Age of Entitlement.* Free Press, 2009.

PART THREE: UNDERSTANDING GOALS AND PERSONAL ACHIEVEMENT

CHAPTER ELEVEN: ALCHEMICAL SUCCESS: THE INFLUENCE OF PERSONAL AURA

Variety 500. *Variety Magazine.* https://variety.com/exec/steve-lafferty/

CHAPTER THIRTEEN: THE ROLE OF STRUCTURE
IN SELF-ACTUALIZATION AND HAPPINESS

Table 7, "Survival of private sector establishments by opening year." US Bureau of Labor Statistics. Accessed September 16, 2023. www.bls.gov/bdm/us_age_naics_00_table7.txt

PART FOUR: DEALING WITH CONFLICT AND
STRUGGLE

CHAPTER FOURTEEN: COUNTER CONFLICT AND
THE HUMAN EXPERIENCE

Tomasello, M. "The ultra-social animal." *Eur. J. Soc. Psychol.* 44 (2014): 187–
194. https://doi.org/10.1002/ejsp.2015

Axelrod, Robert, and Hamilton, William D. "The Evolution of Cooperation." *Science* 211,1390-1396 (1981). https://www.science.org/doi/10.1126/science.7466396

Beck A.T., Rush A.J., Shaw B.F., and Emery, G. *Cognitive Therapy of Depression.* New York: Guilford Press, 1979.

Gottman, John, Katz, Lynn, and Hooven, Carole. "Parental Meta-Emotion Philosophy and the Emotional Life of Families: Theoretical Models and Preliminary Data." *Journal of Family Psychology* 10, (1996): 243–268.

Flavell, J. H. "Metacognition and Cognitive Monitoring: A New Area of Cognitive-Developmental Inquiry." *American Psychologist* 34, (1979): 906–911. https://doi.org/10.1037/0003-066X.34.10.906

Oppezzo, Marily, and Schwartz, Daniel. "Give Your Ideas Some Legs: The Positive Effect of Walking on Creative Thinking." *Journal of Psychology Learning Memory and Cognition* 40, (2014). https://psycnet.apa.org/doiLanding?doi=10.1037%2Fa0036577

Piliavin J.A., and Siegl, E. "Health benefits of volunteering in the Wisconsin longitudinal study." *Journal of Health Soc Behav* 48, no. 4 (2007): 450–64.

Antshel, K.M., and Barkley, R. "Psychosocial interventions in attention deficit hyperactivity disorder." *Child Adolesc Psychiatr Clin N Am* 17, no. 2 (2008): 421–37, x. https://pubmed.ncbi.nlm.nih.gov/18295154/

Fehr, E. and Gächter, S. "Altruistic punishment in humans." *Nature* 415, (2002): 137–40. https://www.nature.com/articles/415137a

Scheff, T.J. "Shame in Self and Society." *Symbolic Interaction* 26, (2003): 239–262. https://doi.org/10.1525/si.2003.26.2.239

Cak, Tuna, H., Caluser, Ilinca, Swain, and James, E. "The Neuroscience Of Human Relationships: Attachment And The Developing Social Brain (2nd edition). Louis Cozolino, W. W. Norton & Company; Second Edition edition, 2014, 656 pp, ISBN-10: 0393707822, ISBN-

13: 978-0393707823." *Infant Mental Health Journal* 36, (2015): 533–535. 10.1002/imhj.21532.

CHAPTER FIFTEEN: THE DUAL EDGE OF SUFFERING AND EXISTENTIAL AWARENESS: A COMPARATIVE STUDY OF HUMAN AND ANIMAL EXISTENCE

McGregor, I., and Little, B.R. "Personal projects, happiness, and meaning: on doing well and being yourself." *J Pers Soc Psychol* 74, no. 2 (1998): 494–512. https://psycnet.apa.org/record/1997-38975-016

CHAPTER SEVENTEEN: OF MICE, MEN, AND JARS OF FLIES - UNDERSTANDING SOCIETAL WELLNESS THROUGH STRUGGLE

John B Calhoun's mouse utopia experiment https://fee.org/articles/john-b-calhoun-s-mouse-utopia-experiment-and-reflections-on-the-welfare-state/?gclid=CjwKCAjw36GjBhAkEi-wAKwIWycV6zOjd2ZiFPtAa_BdyV5KDmlO-oQREdqtA26yMC_l_rkpmSL8iO-hoC9cUQAvD_BwE

Jerry Cantrell's citation of a grade school experiment https://web.ar-chive.org/web/20060908104541/http://users.star-gate.net/~holliday/INT4.HTM

https://medium.com/@worstonlinedater/tinder-experi-ments-ii-guys-unless-you-are-really-hot-you-are-prob-ably-better-off-not-wasting-your-2ddf370a6e9a

https://www.pewresearch.org/social-
trends/2017/12/05/americans-see-different-expec-
tations-for-men-and-women/

CHAPTER EIGHTEEN: THE LIMITS OF LIBERTY

Lukianoff, and Haidt, *The Coddling of the American Mind: How Good Intentions and Bad Ideas Are Setting Up a Generation for Failure.* Penguin Press, 2018.

PART FIVE: SOCIETY, CULTURE, AND THE INDIVIDUAL

CHAPTER TWENTY-THREE: THE IDEOLOGICAL VULNERABILITY OF PRIVILEGE: AN EXAMINATION OF "WHITE GUILT"

Branscombe, N. R., Schmitt, M. T., and Schiffhauer, K. "Racial attitudes in response to thoughts of white privilege." *European Journal of Social Psychology* 37, no. 2 (2007): 203–215.

CHAPTER TWENTY-FOUR: THE COMPLEXITY OF TRANSGENDERISM AND THE INTERPLAY OF SOCIETAL FORCES

Schilt, K., and Westbrook, L. "Doing Gender, Doing Heteronormativity: 'Gender Normals,' Transgender People, and the Social Maintenance of Heterosexuality." *Gender & Society* 23, no. 4 (2009): 440–464. https://doi.org/10.1177/0891243209340034

Beemyn, G., and Rankin, S. *The Lives of Transgender People*. Columbia University Press, 2011.
http://www.jstor.org/stable/10.7312/beem14306

Cooper, B. "Intersectionality." In *The Oxford Handbook of Feminist Theory*. Oxford University Press, 2016.

Nagoshi, J.L., and Brzuzy, S. "Transgender theory: Embodying research and practice." *Affilia* 25, no. 4 (2010): 431–443.

Loomes, R., Hull, L., and Mandy, W. P. L. "What Is the Male-to-Female Ratio in Autism Spectrum Disorder? A Systematic Review and Meta-Analysis." *Journal of the American Academy of Child and Adolescent Psychiatry* 56, no. 6 (2017): 466–474.
https://doi.org/10.1016/j.jaac.2017.03.013

Werling, D.M., and Geschwind, D.H. "Sex differences in autism spectrum disorders." *Current Opinion in Neurology* 26, no. 2 (2013): 146–153.
https://doi.org/10.1097/WCO.0b013e32835ee548

Baron-Cohen, S. "The extreme male brain theory of autism." *Trends in Cognitive Sciences* 6, no. 6 (2002): 248–254.

Archer, J. "Sex differences in aggression in real-world settings: A meta-analytic review." *Review of General Psychology* 8, no. 4 (2004): 291–322.

Deary, I.J., Irwing, P., Der, G., and Bates, T.C. "Brother-sister differences in the g factor in intelligence: Analysis of full, opposite-sex siblings from the NLSY 1979." *Intelligence* 35, no. 5 (2007): 451–456.

Denson, T.F., Mehta, P.H., and Ho Tan, D. "Endogenous testosterone and cortisol jointly influence reactive aggression in women." *Psychoneuroendocrinology* 38, no. 3 (2013): 416–424.

Fiske, S. T., Cuddy, A. J., Glick, P., and Xu, J. "A model of (often mixed) stereotype content: competence and warmth respectively follow from perceived status and competition." *Journal of Personality and Social Psychology* 82, no. 6 (2002): 878.

PART SIX: THE INTERSECTION OF MEDICINE, ETHICS, AND SOCIETY

CHAPTER TWENTY-NINE: HISTORICAL ECHOES: THE LOBOTOMY AND GENDER TRANSITION PROCEDURES

El-Hai, J. *The Lobotomist: A Maverick Medical Genius and His Tragic Quest to Rid the World of Mental Illness.* Wiley, 2005.

Diefenbach, G. J., Diefenbach, D., Baumeister, A., and West, M. "Portrayal of lobotomy in the popular press: 1935–1960." *Journal of the History of the Neurosciences* 8, no. 1(1999): 60–69.

Pressman, J. D. *Last Resort: Psychosurgery and the Limits of Medicine.* Cambridge University Press, 1998.

CHAPTER THIRTY: MASS SOCIOGENIC ILLNESS, THE PLACEBO EFFECT, AND AMERICAN SOCIETY: A COMPLEX TAPESTRY OF MIND AND CULTURE

Weir, E. "Mass sociogenic illness." *CMAJ* 172, no. 1 (2005): 36. doi: 10.1503/cmaj.045027

Slife, Brent. "Taking Practice Seriously: Toward a Relational Ontology." *Journal of Theoretical and Philosophical Psychology* 24, (2004): 157–178. 10.1037/h0091239.

Moyers, T.B., and Miller, W.R. "Is low therapist empathy toxic?" *Psychol Addict Behav* 27, no. 3 (2013): 878–84. Doi: 10.1037/a0030274. Epub 2012 Oct 1.

Shedler, J. "Where Is the Evidence for 'Evidence-Based' Therapy?" *Psychiatr Clin North Am* 41, no. 2 (2018): 319–329. doi: 10.1016/j.psc.2018.02.001.

Gaudiano, B.A., Nowlan, K., Brown, L.A., Epstein-Lubow, G., and Miller, I.W. "An open trial of a new acceptance-based behavioral treatment for major depression with psychotic features." *Behav Modif* 37, no. 3 (2013): 324–55. doi: 10.1177/0145445512465173. Epub 2012 Dec 6.

https://www.apa.org/pubs/reports/2015-report.pdf

Howick, J., Friedemann, C., Tsakok, M., Watson, R., Tsakok, T., Thomas, J., Perera, R., Fleming, S., and Heneghan, C. "Are treatments more effective than placebos? A systematic review and meta-analysis." *PLoS One* 8, no. 5 (2013): e62599. doi: 10.1371/journal.pone.0062599. Erratum in: PLoS One. 2016;11(1):e0147354.

Rüsch, N., Zlati, A., Black, G., and Thornicroft, G. "Does the stigma of mental illness contribute to suicidality?" *The British Journal of Psychiatry: The Journal of*

Mental Science 205, no. 4 (2014): 257–259.
https://doi.org/10.1192/bjp.bp.114.145755

PART SEVEN: ILLUMINATING UNCONVENTIONAL WISDOM

CHAPTER THIRTY-THREE: AN ILLUMINATION OF UNCONVENTIONAL BRILLIANCE

https://templeos.org/

Hicks, J. "God's Lonely Programmer." Vice.com
https://www.vice.com/en/article/wnj43x/gods-lonely-programmer

CHAPTER THIRTY-FOUR: BIRTH OF BRILLIANCE: UNRAVELING THE MYSTERIES OF THE CREATIVE PROCESS

Les Claypool discussing the innate musicality nuances of Stewart Copeland https://youtu.be/aPNmqNtZi20

PART EIGHT: EXPLORING COMPLEX IDEAS

CHAPTER THIRTY-SEVEN: CAUSALITY, FREE WILL, AND THE INFINITE LIBRARY

Gardner, M. "The fantastic combinations of John Conway's new solitaire game 'life.'" *Scientific American* 223, no. 4 (1970): 120–123.

Borges, J. L. "The Library of Babel." Editorial Sur, 1941.

CHAPTER FORTY: STATISTICAL MANIPULATION: PERVERTING THE ODDS

Arnett, J. "Reckless behavior in adolescence: A developmental perspective." *Developmental Review* 12, no. 4, (1992): 339–373. https://doi.org/10.1016/0273-2297(92)90013-R

CHAPTER FORTY-THREE: A HEGELIAN PERSPECTIVE

Voyer, D., Voyer, S., and Bryden, M.P. "Magnitude of sex differences in spatial abilities: A meta-analysis and consideration of critical variables." *Psychological Bulletin* 117, no. 2 (1995): 250–270. https://doi.org/10.1037/0033-2909.117.2.250

PART NINE: FUTURE OUTLOOKS AND TRANSITIONS

CHAPTER FORTY-FOUR: THE INADVERTENT EXODUS: WHEN ARTIFICIAL INTELLIGENCE USURPS HUMAN SKILLS

https://sgp.fas.org/crs/natsec/R45178.pdf

David M. J., Lazer et al. "The science of fake news." *Science* 359, no. 6380 (2018): 1094–1096. https://www.science.org/doi/10.1126/science.aao2998

CHAPTER FORTY-SEVEN: THE FULFILLMENT TRIAD

Chetty, Raj, Hendren, Nathaniel, Kline, Patrick, and Saez, Emmanuel. "Where is the land of Opportunity? The Geography of Intergenerational Mobility in the

United States." *The Quarterly Journal of Economics* 129, no. 4 (2014): 1553–1623. https://doi.org/10.1093/qje/qju022

Ericsson, K.A., Krampe, R.T., and Tesch-Römer, C. "The role of deliberate practice in the acquisition of expert performance." *Psychological Review* 100, no. 3 (1993): 363–406. https://doi.org/10.1037/0033-295X.100.3.363

Melograni, P. *Wolfgang Amadeus Mozart: A Biography*. Chicago: University of Chicago Press, 2007.

Hershbein, Brad, and Kahn, Lisa B. "Do Recessions Accelerate Routine-Biased Technological Change? Evidence from Vacancy Postings." *American Economic Review* 108, no. 7 (2018): 1737–72.

Granovetter, M.S. "The Strength of Weak Ties." *American Journal of Sociology* 78, no. 6 (1973): 1360–1380. http://www.jstor.org/stable/2776392

Vallerand, R.J., Blanchard, C., Mageau, G.A., Koestner, R., Ratelle, C., Léonard, M., Gagné, M., and Marsolais, J. "Les passions de l'âme: On obsessive and harmonious passion." *Journal of Personality and Social Psychology* 85, no. 4 (2003): 756–767. https://doi.org/10.1037/0022-3514.85.4.756

CHAPTER FORTY-EIGHT: DIGITAL PARADIGM

Goldhaber, M.H. "The attention economy and the Net." *First Monday* 2, no. 4 (1997).

Eich, B., & Bondy, B. "Basic Attention Token (BAT): Block-chain Based Digital Advertising." *Basic Attention Token White Paper*, (2018).

Brame, C. J. "Effective Educational Videos: Principles and Guidelines for Maximizing Student Learning from Video Content." *CBE life sciences education* 15, no. 4 (2016). es6. https://doi.org/10.1187/cbe.16-03-0125

Turkle, S. *Alone Together: Why We Expect More from Technology and Less from Each Other.* Basic Books, 2011.